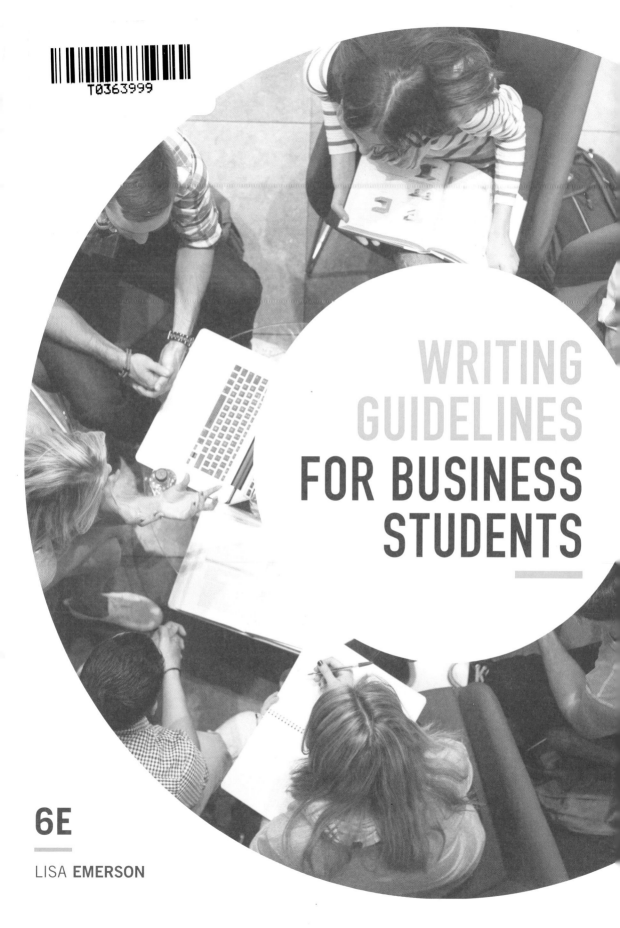

WRITING GUIDELINES
FOR BUSINESS STUDENTS

6E

LISA **EMERSON**

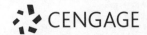

Writing Guidelines for Business Students
6th Edition
Lisa Emerson

Portfolio lead: Fiona Hammond
Product manager: Rachael Pictor
Content developer: Emily Spurr
Project editor: Sutha Surenddar
Editor: Anne Mulvaney
Proofreader: Julie Wicks
Permissions/Photo researcher: Wendy Duncan
Cover designer: Cengage Creative Studio
Text designer: Rina Gargano
Cover: Getty Images/Clerkenwell
KnowledgeWorks Global Ltd.

Any URLs contained in this publication were checked for
currency during the production process. Note, however, that the
publisher cannot vouch for the ongoing currency of URLs.

For product information and technology assistance,
in Australia call 1300 790 853;
in New Zealand call 0800 449 725

For permission to use material from this text or product, please email
aust.permissions@cengage.com

National Library of Australia Cataloguing-in-Publication Data
Author: Emerson, Lisa.
Title: Writing guidelines for business students / Lisa Emerson.
Edition: 6th ed.
ISBN: 9780170454377 (pbk.)
Notes: Includes bibliographical references.
Subjects:
  Business report writing.
  Business--Study and teaching.

Cengage Learning Australia
Level 7, 80 Dorcas Street
South Melbourne, Victoria Australia 3205

Cengage Learning New Zealand
Unit 4B Rosedale Office Park
331 Rosedale Road, Albany, North Shore 0632, NZ

For learning solutions, visit cengage.com.au

Printed in China by 1010 Printing International Limited.
1 2 3 4 5 6 7 25 24 23 22 21

Contents

About the author

Lisa Emerson is the Director of Teaching and Learning in the College of Humanities and Social Sciences, Massey University and Professor of Teaching and Learning in Higher Education. Her fields of research are academic writing, information literacy and the transition to higher education. She is a former Fulbright scholar, and winner of the New Zealand Prime Minister's Award for Sustained Excellence in Tertiary Teaching.

Notes on the sixth edition

The sixth edition of *Writing Guidelines for Business Students* was written during a global pandemic and an information crisis, which are threatening the future of the entire world, with impacts on the future of democracy and the business world. Other major world issues, such as the climate crisis, are also impacting on how we do business ethically and with attention to sustainability. Now, more than ever, we need to support the creative, innovative business leaders of the future by supporting students who are studying in business and commerce fields. This book is written for you, as one of the next generation of leaders and innovators, by providing you with guidance on the requirements of assessment.

Times of economic hardship usually lead to increased enrolments in higher education, as more school leavers, and also people who have been affected professionally by economic circumstances, realise the importance of further training. I have designed this book to be of use to all new students – but I also intend it to be of use to those who have been away from study for some time.

There are two significant changes to this edition of this book: one is the updating of Chapter 13 to reflect the requirements of the 7th edition of APA referencing style, with more detail on referencing online sources. The other is a new chapter, Chapter 5, 'Thinking about assessment and group work' – this is important because, as teachers in higher education have thought more broadly about assessment in line with current research indicators of best practice, new genres of assessment are emerging that may be unfamiliar to most students. This chapter enables students to think about what is required in any unfamiliar genre and make wise decisions. Other chapters have been substantially rewritten – especially Chapter 3 – to reflect the online environment we are all working in. All chapters have been revised: there have been many technological changes, and changes in how we deliver tertiary education since the last edition, and my aim has been to reflect the most significant of those changes in this edition. I would like to acknowledge Katherine Chisholm for her writing of Chapter 3, and Bruce MacKay for his writing of Chapter 9, 'Writing for the web', and Appendix C. Mike Brennan and Grant Harris wrote chapters on note taking and writing research proposals and research reports in earlier editions of this book, and their drafts have influenced the rewritten versions of those chapters in this edition. My thanks are due also to Emily Spurr, Rachael Pictor, Sutha Surenddar and Anne Mulvaney at Cengage, who have supported me, with deft professional skill, and much patience and personal encouragement, through the revision of the text during this difficult time when COVID-19 upended all our lives. I consider myself very fortunate to be working with such an enabling and encouraging editorial team.

Finally, the book is dedicated to my children, Edward, Rose, Emily and Lizzy, who have inspired me to make a difference. In particular, my daughter Emily is attending her first year of university study this year, and her questions, concerns and excitement have made me all the more aware of the challenges and significance of the transition to higher education.

LISA EMERSON
March 2021

Publisher's note

The author and Cengage Learning would like to thank the following reviewers for their incisive and helpful feedback:

- Morag Burnie – The University of Melbourne
- Michelle Cull – Western Sydney University
- Kim Love – University of Auckland
- Imad Moosa – RMIT University

We would also like to thank the following contributors:

- Dr Bruce MacKay, who wrote Chapter 9 and Appendix C
- Katherine Chisholm, who wrote Chapter 3

Introduction

Business students are very often assessed on the basis of written work. The main purpose of this guide is to provide an introduction to writing assignments in a business or commerce department.

Lecturers may ask you to produce many different types of assignments. You may be familiar with writing essays from school days, but reports, case studies, literature reviews, web pages and e-portfolios may be new tasks. These different formats allow you to develop different skills; the following are examples of skills involved in different formats:

- Essays test your ability to construct a logical argument, usually about an abstract or theoretical issue.
- Reports and case studies require you to apply concepts and theoretical models to practical situations.
- Literature reviews develop your skills in understanding, organising and synthesising what other academics have written on a particular topic.
- E-portfolios or journals encourage you to reflect on your learning as a way of going deeper into the course material.

These various formats are described in detail in the middle chapters of this book. The earlier chapters focus on the research and writing processes. The appendices pursue more specialised aspects of writing assignments and should be used as reference materials.

This book is intended as a guide. If assignment requirements do not appear to fit the formats described here, read Chapter 5 carefully for some approaches you might take but, if in doubt, do not hesitate to consult your lecturer or tutor. Some teachers will be prepared to provide exemplars, but others may prefer you just to work from the instructions. Be flexible and prepared to adapt your format to suit the specific requirements of different courses and teachers.

1.1 Assignment presentation

Individual courses may have different procedures; always check the course outline or assignment directions.

Professional appearance

Students often underestimate the value of presenting their work well; this is a mistake. The visual impact of your assignment *does* influence your marker(s). You are undergoing professional training; for this reason, the person marking your work will expect you to produce work that would appear credible in the work environment. You do not want your writing to convey the impression that you are a careless person.

Do not fill the entire page, solidly, with print. Set off the print with lots of white space; your assignment will be easier to read and important points will stand out.

The use of numbered headings, subheadings, tables, diagrams and graphs all improve the appearance of a written project. It is important to be consistent in the use of formatting techniques, such as section headings, and in the way graphs and tables are presented within a report (see Appendix C on presenting data).

Most assignments should have a title page, and it is also a good idea to have your name and ID number in the header or footer. Always include page numbers.

Leave a 3 cm space along the left-hand margin of each page of your assignment.

The text should be 1.5 or double spaced to enhance readability.

1.2   Responsibility for taking a copy

There is always a risk of an assignment being lost. Save your document carefully and often, and upload a copy of your assignment to an online drive before submitting for marking. Better yet, do your work in an online space such as Google Drive. Printing out a hard copy is also recommended. If your assignment is misplaced and you have not made a copy, you will have to rewrite the assignment or forfeit the marks: the responsibility to make a copy is *yours*.

1.3   Correct use of English

Like the visual appearance of your work, the correctness of your grammar, word usage, punctuation and spelling will influence the marker. In some courses a percentage of the mark is given for language use. For tertiary-level work you are expected to understand and apply the basic rules of English. If you have problems with writing, consult reference books (from a library) on English grammar and style or find a good-quality website (such as the Purdue OWL or Massey OWLL – these are easily found through a Google search), or perhaps contact a support person on your campus. Alternatively, you may want to use a website such as Grammarly to improve your writing style.

Even if you have good English skills, you need to take the time to proofread your work. Spelling and other types of careless mistakes distract the marker and diminish their sense of your professionalism. Don't depend on a spell-checker alone – it does not pick up all mistakes!

1.4   Plagiarism

Copying another person's ideas or words without acknowledgement (i.e. plagiarism) or without correct referencing is a grave academic and legal offence. It is viewed very seriously and the penalties can be severe. Discuss your assignments with fellow students by all means, but the work you submit for marking must be your own work. If you want to include someone else's work directly into your assignment, the author and original source of this work must be clearly shown. See Chapter 13 and Appendix A for more information on acknowledging other sources and avoiding plagiarism.

It is important, too, that you do not enable plagiarism by others. For example, if another student asks to see your assignment 'to get some ideas about what's needed', and you send the assignment to them electronically, it is very easy for them to adapt it and submit it as their own. You should never send an assessment electronically to another student, because once you do this, you have no control over that document. Even if the person you have sent it to respects your work and does not plagiarise, there is nothing to stop them sending it onto someone else – someone you might not even know – who may plagiarise your work. If another student asks to see your work and you want to help, print out a copy and let them read it while you are present: do not leave the assignment with them.

Many institutions submit assignments through text-checking software such as Turnitin, which is a text-matching program that identifies copied text. Always check your score, and if you have any questions about the results, contact your teacher.

1.5   References

For most assignments you will need to consult articles, books and other published materials. The list of references you use in compiling your work should be attached to the assignment (see Chapter 13 for details on how this list should be formatted).

1.6   Handing in assignments

Most courses specify due dates for assignments. While an online or phone-based planner is convenient, it is useful to have an annual planner that can allow you to see the spacing of your various commitments (including all assignments and tests) so you can plan ahead for those times when you have multiple assignments due at the same time, such as at the end of semester or just before the mid-semester break. Buy yourself a wall planner and, as soon as you are provided with these due dates, plot them on the planner. Try not to fall behind with assignments. Some lecturers and tutors do not accept late assignments; others take off a percentage of the mark for work submitted late. But even if no penalty exists for late assignments, you should pace your work so that you do not get out of step with other work. If, despite your best efforts, you are falling behind and will need an extension, contact your tutor *before* the due date.

1.7   Responding to your grade

When your assignment comes back, you will be keen to see the grade. If you received a passing or high grade, well done! Time to celebrate.

But sometimes you will be disappointed in a grade. You will feel that you worked very hard, so it's difficult to understand why your marker didn't feel you met the mark. Don't be discouraged! Keep in mind that grades are not determined by effort but are measured against a set of criteria. This grade says nothing about who you are as a person or how far you will go in life, it is simply an assessment of understanding at a very early point in your learning journey. Grades give you summative feedback on where there are gaps in your learning so that you have the chance to improve on these as you progress with your studies. It is only one assessment in a lifetime of wonderful achievements to come. Use a growth mindset to process the feedback and then dig into your learning to improve. Emotional intelligence is key to processing disappointing results.

If you really feel your marks are unfair, it is reasonable to approach your teacher and ask for more feedback or a reconsideration of the grade. But wait at least 24 hours before you do this. Giving yourself time to breathe and think means you can avoid sending your teacher (or at some point, your boss) an emotive email filled with angry disappointment that states you are unhappy and they are unfair. Read the feedback carefully to see if you can understand why you have lost marks. Look at the grading criteria. Try to understand the problem first. And then, if you do decide to approach your teacher for more information, do so in a calm manner: explain why you're concerned ('I don't see, according to the criteria, where I have missed the marks here', *not* 'I worked really hard on this and this isn't fair!').

1.8   Read the feedback

Students tend to undervalue the feedback that is given to them when an assignment is returned. We're so focused on the grade that we barely take the time to read what the marker has written. It is very important that you read the feedback, as this is a valuable aid to learning what you may be doing wrong and how you could improve your work. If you don't understand the feedback, or would like more feedback, make an appointment to see your marker or your tutor and ask (politely) for more information. Explain that you want to improve your work. It is their job to provide you with feedback, and they will welcome the questions of a student who genuinely wants to improve their work.

1.9   Online requirements

If you are returning to study after a break from education, you need to be aware that the tertiary environment has changed. Almost all assignments need to be produced and submitted in electronic form. You will need regular access to a computer and high-speed internet access, and you will need competent word processing skills. Most courses are now taught, at least partially, through an online classroom, where readings and activities are posted, and ideas relating to the course can be discussed with the teacher and other students. Many courses require assignments to be submitted online for assessment or for peer review, or require a minimum engagement with online discussion. If your typing skills are not strong, you might want to look up free typing lessons or free typing skills programs online to improve your keyboard skills.

1.10 Learning and writing support

Your institution is likely to have learning and writing support tutors available on campus and/or online to help you with the writing of assignments. You should identify and locate these support services as soon as possible. If you're struggling with assignment writing, or if you just want to improve your grades, you are strongly advised to make use of their services. Many support services allow you to bring along the draft of an assignment, or an assignment topic, and then work with a tutor to improve your writing, your understanding of the conventions of academic writing and your writing process. There is no stigma in using these services: in fact, many high-achieving students attribute their success to working with writing tutors for some of their assignments. For a visit to a writing tutor, you will probably need to book ahead, so don't wait for a crisis.

2 On being a business student

Most business or commerce students are focused on a practical outcome of their degree, such as a foothold into a profession, a step up the career ladder or an opportunity to influence the future or take a new direction, and also the positive spin-offs of a successful professional life (e.g. wealth or influence). It is important to keep your practical goals in focus while you are studying. A degree, diploma or certificate is no guarantee of a successful professional life. But the learning you acquire during your studies is the key to future success. A 'Cs make degrees' attitude does not make any sense in a business context: what you learn during tertiary study will make a huge difference to your capacity to achieve your goals, and so *learning* needs to be the focus of your attention and effort.

Furthermore, as a business student, you should look to attain value for your investment in education, and the mere achievement of a qualification doesn't constitute value. You need to gather knowledge, capacity, skills, networks and more, because engaging in an active, goal-focused way is a key step towards your success.

2.1 Teaching staff

If you have come straight from school, you may be tempted to assume that lecturers and tutors will play the same role as your teachers at school. But let's be very clear about this: they won't. While school teachers are likely to know your name, follow up on late assignments, notice if you're performing below your potential, ask you why you weren't in class and address poor behaviour, a university lecturer (or other tertiary teacher) may not do any of these things.

Instead, a tertiary teacher assumes that, because you have chosen to study at tertiary level, you will take responsibility for your own learning. This means it is up to you to turn up to class, do your research and study, hand in assignments on time, and ensure you know when and where exams and tests will take place. If you don't do these things, no-one is going to check up on you.

You need, therefore, to start tertiary study seeing yourself as, and behaving like, an independent learner. If you know your time management skills are poor or you don't know how to locate quality information, then you need to upskill. Most tertiary institutions have courses on time management, library skills and study skills; take advantage of these opportunities and make sure you acquire the skills you need.

KNOW YOUR WEAKNESSES

TIP

Being honest with yourself will enable you to seek help to develop new skills.

While your tertiary teachers will take on a different role from other teachers you've encountered before, they are still there to help you. Most lecturers have office hours; if you're struggling, they will be happy to help, but it's up to you to take the initiative to visit them. If you're a distance student, you can email the teacher or post a query on a course website, and you should expect a prompt response (24 to 48 working hours).

2.2 Being an independent learner in business

To be an independent learner, you don't just need particular skills, you also need a certain attitude to learning which is built on key characteristics:

* *Curiosity*. You must develop an interest in what you're studying. Curious people want to explore ideas, ask questions and find answers. They want to know what other people think about a topic. They want to know the point of a lecture or reading; they want to know what motivates certain points of view. Curious people read and listen with questions on their minds. Whatever you're studying now will be useful in the future – even if that is not immediately apparent – so look for the interest factor and engage.

* *An interest in the wider context of business*. Becoming successful in business isn't just about what you're learning in class – it's about applying that learning to what you see happening in the outside world. You need to start this now. Read the news from a range of sources, and identify thought leaders in your field and keep up with what they're saying, so that you're constantly gathering information about the world (and the world of business). This knowledge and the ability to continually gather and reflect on current business information, thinking and events is the key to good business analysis and a critical ingredient for entrepreneurial and innovative mindsets. Start now and make keeping in touch with new ideas (and reflecting on how your new learning relates to those ideas) a regular part of your routine.

* *Willingness to change*. A successful learner is ready to change their ideas, views and ways of thinking. They relish challenges to old assumptions. They're prepared to change not only what they think but who they are. This is often an uncomfortable situation: change is not easy. But if you're not open to change, you can't learn. Of course, you should still test the ideas, skills and theories you're learning against any 'real life' experience you have, but do so with an open, critical mind.

KNOW YOURSELF

TIP

Become aware of the key ideas and assumptions you bring to university. By being aware of these ideas, you will be more open to new ideas and/or changing old ones.

* *Focus*. There are lots of distractions in a student's life: their personal lives, family problems, friends, financial issues, jobs and all the new experiences that come with

being a student. We also live with endless distractions from social media and other online activities. But if you are to succeed in study, you must learn to focus. Play when you're playing, but when it's time to study you need to spend time on-task. You need to be able to eliminate distractions and focus on what needs to be done. Poor students sit in a lecture and check their Facebook page. Successful students know there is no point in being in a lecture or engaging with online learning material unless they are fully focused.

- *Responsibility*. No-one is responsible for your success but you.
- *Organisation*. This matters on a number of levels. If you are an internal student, you need to be able to get out of bed in time for class, arrive at class with the right materials, hand in assignments on time and do the necessary study. If you're studying while working, or studying and juggling a busy family life, you have special challenges and will need to be intentional about carving out regular time for study in a quiet space. But you also need to be able to sort important from peripheral material, identify useful sources of information, identify the key ideas in a lecture or reading and see what really matters.

TIP

WALL PLANNERS

Buy a wall planner and enter in the dates of all assessments (assignments, tests and exams) plus semester dates. This way you can see your deadlines in advance.

- *Energy*. You need to have the energy to push yourself beyond your limits. Sometimes you will have to work late after a demanding day to meet a deadline. Study is hard work, often it is an endurance task: are you up for that?
- *Rest*. Stress can be a big problem for students. This is partly because of the demands and complexity of study, but also because, unlike a nine-to-five job, there is no time of the week where you can say everything is done. You could always study more. But if you're not going to be overcome by stress and exhaustion, you have to intentionally build time to rest and relax into your week.

The great thing about all these characteristics is that they will be invaluable not only for your study but also in the business world. If you don't feel confident that you have these characteristics, start working on them now. Read this list often to remind yourself to persevere.

2.3 Writing assignments

We turn now to what you need to know about written assessment and the skills required to write assignments in business. In many ways, these skills are similar to the skills required by students in other disciplines. But because business is an applied and vocationally relevant discipline, extra skills are required that apply knowledge to real-life contexts. These include formative and summative assessment. It is common now for courses to include both formative and summative assessment (see Figure 2.1).

Formative assessment	Includes assignments and activities that provide feedback on your learning but do not contribute to your final grade (such as online quizzes and peer and tutor reviews).
Summative assessment	Includes all assignments and tests that contribute to your final grade.

Figure 2.1 Formative and summative assessment

Formative assessment focuses on enabling your learning; summative assessment focuses on assessing your learning.

It is tempting to focus primarily on summative assessment; after all, this is where the marks are. But recall our earlier comments, that the focus of tertiary education is learning for a future in the business world: seen this way, formative assessment will be just as important as summative assessment. It aims to improve your learning and help you to feel confident that you understand the course material. Always take any opportunity to do formative assessment activities; they will contribute to your success in the long run.

Other skills required to apply knowledge to real-life contexts are as follows:

- *Writing matters*. Your ideas can't come across clearly if you're not writing clearly. Put effort into your writing and presentation: edit and proofread, ask someone else to proofread your work, present your work professionally and, if you're not confident about your writing, contact support services. Writing affects your credibility: a reader will think that you are a careless person if your work is full of errors. Your writing skills also affect your employability. Every year there are articles in the media deploring university graduates' poor writing skills. Tertiary study is a place to develop new, more sophisticated writing skills.

- *Writing for a reader*. It's easy to forget, but someone is going to read your assignment. Write with the reader in mind. What are they looking for? Look at the assignment topic and instructions carefully and make sure you understand what they're wanting from you. Is there a marking schedule? This provides valuable insights into the issues you must cover and how the assignment will be marked. Other questions to consider are: how can you make your writing interesting for the reader? How can you make the logic of what you're saying clear? How can you make your assignment stand out from the crowd? Reshape and edit your work with your reader in mind.

- *Structure matters*. Assignments come in different forms: reports, essays, briefing papers, journals and research papers. It is important to write in the format specified in the assignment instructions, and if you're not sure about this, ask for clarification. Many of these formats, such as reports, seminars and research papers, will be found in your future workplace, so learn them now.

- *Match the information needs of each assignment.* Some forms of assessment require you to use only academic sources (e.g. peer-reviewed articles), but others require you to use professional sources (e.g. company reports, professional journals) and current media sources. Make sure you know what kind of information is required for an assignment and that you know how to locate appropriate sources.
- *Going beyond Google for academic sources.* There's no doubt that Google has revolutionised how we find information. And maybe you will start information searches with a look at Google. But it's often important to use quality, peer-reviewed information for your assignments, so it is vital that you learn how to use Google Scholar and search academic databases. Ask a librarian to show you how or attend a library orientation session at your institution.
- *Going beyond description.* Because knowledge is changing so quickly, most tertiary environments focus not on filling your head with knowledge, but enabling you to evaluate and critique information, and to come to conclusions about a particular question, problem or issue. It is important when writing assignments not just to describe what other people have said and found, but to critique these ideas. This means looking at the strengths and weaknesses of their evidence or ideas and coming to a conclusion about the value or validity of what they're saying.
- *Developing higher-level thinking skills.* Assignments may ask you to analyse, evaluate or compare and contrast different ideas or situations. These instructions require you to use higher-level reasoning skills. Details of some key words that indicate higher-order thinking are provided in Table 2.1.

Table 2.1 Common key words indicating tasks that require higher-level reasoning skills

Key word	What this word means in an assignment
Evaluate	Consider the value of an idea, situation or solution in the light of evidence
Compare and contrast	Examine what two ideas, institutions or situations have in common – and how they differ
Analyse	Look at and critique the component parts of an idea, problem or situation
Discuss	Discuss the pros and cons of an idea/concept and come to a conclusion
Argue	Present a case backed up by evidence
Examine	Investigate closely. Look closely at the components of a situation or idea

- *Learning from your mistakes.* In any business context you have to both critique your own performance and learn from feedback (e.g. from clients and managers). Therefore, a vital part of assignments is learning from your mistakes (i.e. reading the feedback). For any assignment except an A+ your tutor should have indicated how you could have improved your grade. If they haven't done so, or haven't given enough detail, ask (nicely) for more feedback. Value and learn from the feedback you are given.

2.4   Conclusion

We said earlier that tertiary education is an investment in the future. But it is important to think about what kind of investment this is. Students often, because they pay fees, see themselves as customers or clients of the university or tertiary provider. This is true to some extent, but the idea of being a customer can be somewhat misleading.

Paying fees to a tertiary institution does not mean you can passively sit back and be provided with what you need: it is not like going to McDonald's and purchasing a meal. It is more like purchasing a subscription to the gym. Just as the gym is obliged to provide you with good-quality equipment and qualified and experienced trainers, so a tertiary provider is obliged to provide you with good learning resources and qualified and experienced teachers. But no-one buys membership of a gym and then expects to be pronounced fit and healthy; instead, it is up to the client to use the equipment and trainers wisely and commit to the work that will help them to achieve their fitness goals. So it is with study: paying for access to tertiary resources doesn't make you educated or fit for work; only wise use of resources and commitment to the work will lead to results. It really is over to you.

Check your understanding

1. What are you hoping to achieve through studying?
2. How do you think learning in a tertiary institution is different from learning at school or in the workplace? Why do you think it is different?
3. Look at the list of attitudes that are required of business students. Which attitudes do you already have? Which ones are more difficult for you? What might you do to develop those attitudes?
4. How are summative and formative assessment different? Why might formative assessment be so important?

Helpful resources

How to handle stress, with links to useful resources: https://www.learnpsychology.org/student-stress-anxiety-guide

Time management and how to avoid procrastination: https://www.collegexpress.com/articles-and-advice/majors-and-academics/blog/top-10-ways-avoid-procrastination

Overcoming perfectionism: https://blog.innerdrive.co.uk/student-perfectionism-anxiety-fear-of-failure

How to be a successful student: https://examstudyexpert.com/successful-student-habits

How academic writing differs from school writing: https://open.lib.umn.edu/collegesuccess/chapter/8-1-whats-different-about-college-writing

3 Finding information

Shouldn't finding information be easy? We don't live in a society where information is in short supply. It surrounds us to an astounding degree. It's easy to search for, with Google making suggestions as we start typing or Siri responding to our questions, and it bounces back at us, as sites 'suggested for us' come up on our social media feeds.

It's likely that you've already searched many times for information for personal, education or work reasons, but many students still find the transition to finding information suitable for tertiary level assignments challenging. This chapter aims to help you with this process and will cover:

- the types of information you may need to find as a business student
- the tools you'll use to find them
- searching and strategies to improve search results
- evaluating what you find.

These skills are important components of information literacy, which is the ability to find and evaluate information, synthesise it with existing knowledge, and create and present new information. These are key skills to develop not just as a student, but they're also skills that will be expected by future employers.

3.1 Types of information

Information is created by all sorts of people for all sorts of reasons, including for commercial reasons, to inform and educate, or to entertain. Information is created by professionals and by amateurs. Sadly, information can also be used as a weapon to harm or misinform people. Information can come in different formats, which shape the value and purpose of the information. Understanding the process behind the creation of a piece of information helps us to understand its value to ourselves, and what its benefits and shortcomings might be.

Table 3.1 shows the main different types of information you will interact with as part of your studies.

Table 3.1 Different types of information

Format	Who writes it?	Who is it written for?	Uses	Drawbacks
Book/e-books One of the oldest formats, books can range from novels to textbooks, scholarly to self-help	Academics Businesspeople Creative writers (fiction and non-fiction) Experts	Academics or students Businesspeople The general public Experts or enthusiasts	Can provide both wide coverage of the topic and the details Usually written for a wide audience, so is more accessible	Books take time to produce so are less up-to-date Wide range of types of books means more careful evaluation is needed
Scholarly journal articles Also known as academic, peer-reviewed or research journal articles	Academics and researchers	Academics and researchers	Rigorously reviewed before publication High level of credibility More up-to-date than books	Can be difficult to read as writing style is formal and technical Not written for a student audience May be too detailed or specific
Review articles: a scholarly article which is a review of recent research in an area	Academics and researchers	Academics and researchers	Rigorously reviewed before publication High level of credibility More up-to-date than books	Broader than usual scholarly journal articles Still formal and technical Find in multidisciplinary article databases (see below)
Magazines and newspapers/ online news, online current affairs resources	Journalists	The widest possible audience	Can respond quickly to events Easy to read, can be a good introduction to a topic	Quality variable Not acceptable if scholarly journals are required
Trade and professional magazines	Business journalists, practitioners of a trade, sometimes academics	Businesspeople, other people involved in the trade, industry or profession	Good subject knowledge More up-to-date than scholarly articles Easier to read than scholarly articles	Quality variable Not acceptable if scholarly journals are required

Format	Who writes it?	Who is it written for?	Uses	Drawbacks
Blog posts, podcasts, YouTube videos, social media posts	Varies widely	Varies widely, but usually a general rather than an academic audience	Can be extremely up-to-date Allows more diverse voices, potentially Audio-visual mode can be more engaging	Needs careful evaluation of the creator's expertise Needs checking to ensure it isn't fake news, misinformation or disinformation Tracing the original or complete source from social media posts can be difficult Not defined as scholarly
Official information: • Statistics • Reports	Government departments Non-government organisations (NGOs) – e.g. International Monetary Fund	Citizens Policymakers, politicians, general public	Authoritative Excellent source of information on Australian and New Zealand topics	May require advanced searching to find
Business information: • Market reports • Industry reports • Company reports • Stock market	Individual companies Companies in the business of providing business information (e.g. Bloomberg)	Governments (legal obligations) Other businesses Investors Consumers Entrepreneurs	Authoritative	Much of it is only available behind paywalls May require advanced searching or specialist databases to find

TIP

FAKE NEWS

Fake news is deliberate misinformation that is created with malicious intent. It is often created to look like 'real' news and is easily spread via social media, including by bots. Fake news has existed for centuries but has become a major problem because of the ease and speed with which it can be created and spread via the internet. Among its dangerous effects are exacerbating divisions between different communities and eroding trust in authoritative sources, such as governments, the mainstream press and scientists.

GOOGLE SCHOLAR

Google Scholar acts like a multidisciplinary database, but covers a wider range of academic material, including conference papers, working papers, books and theses. Unlike true databases, there is no human oversight of Google Scholar, so more evaluation is necessary by users. It is very popular with students because it is familiar and easy to search. You may need to access it via your tertiary institution library's website or adjust settings so that you can authenticate and get access to your library's subscribed content.

WIKIPEDIA

One of the most popular sites in the world, Wikipedia is a crowd-sourced encyclopedia. It is often criticised because the writers are effectively anonymous, but information on Wikipedia is usually linked to credible sources. Use these sources for assignments, rather than Wikipedia articles themselves, and if the information isn't referenced, check its validity.

3.2   Picking the good stuff: evaluating sources

Most online searches bring back hundreds, thousands or even millions of results, so one of the big challenges we face is which results to choose. The quality of the different results will also vary widely, so we want to choose the good and avoid the bad. Assess the results you choose by considering:

1   relevance
2   currency
3   authority
4   purpose
5   accuracy.

These five criteria are explained in the following sections.

Relevance

Relevance is perhaps the most basic evaluation criterion of the five. If we do not think that a result is relevant – that is, useful in helping to answer our question – nothing else matters. Relevance has both an objective and a subjective quality. Most databases and search engines display results in 'relevance' order, the result of an algorithm that considers such things as:

• where search terms occur (e.g. in the title or abstract)
• how close together they occur
• how often they occur.

The algorithm may also do things such as favour more recent material and types of information (e.g. books or journal articles), and in the case of search engines, search your history and user profile. This is objective relevance, based on rules that a machine can run. As searchers, we often place a lot of trust in the ability of search engines to get relevance right.

But as searchers, we also assess relevance in a more subjective way. These are the personal factors that lead us to choose a particular result over another – maybe because it's easier to read, or the author's opinions match ours. Research is also a process, and personal relevance can change. A journal article may be too specific when we're starting out, but highly relevant when we know more.

When a librarian helps people search, they bring their expertise in searching to find results that are objectively relevant, but the person they're helping is the only person who can truly judge the relevance of any result in that moment.

Currency

When any piece of information becomes out-of-date will vary wildly and depends on what it is needed for. A company's annual report is technically out-of-date when the next one appears, but it may be still relevant if the reader is looking at trends or the history of the company.

To assess currency, it is important to find out when the information was published, and consider if it is still valid. Ask yourself:

- Is there likely to be a more recent version?
- Do changes in technology, law or the political/social situation mean it is out-of-date?
- Is it theoretical? Descriptions of practice date more than theoretical discussions.
- If it is older, is it an important work or by an important author?
- If it is older, is it useful as historical context?

Publication dates are usually easy to find for books, reports and journal, magazine and newspaper articles. An exception is general website pages, which may not have dates. This does not always mean they are out-of-date, as they may be pages that are updated only when the information needs to change – for example, contact information or opening hours.

Authority

Authority refers to the background of the people providing the information and what that says about whether we can trust it. Authority can come from different places, including:

- lived experience, whether personal or professional
- study and research
- professional expertise.

Essentially, we need to ask: what knowledge sits behind an author's claims? Also, consider whether the information had to go through any kind of quality control, such as editing, fact-checking or peer review. This is the strength of academic material because the peer review process is so rigorous.

Sometimes the authority attaches to an organisation as well as, or instead of, the author, so consider that too. For example, is the organisation putting out the information well-known and respected, and what are its aims?

Books and articles will usually include some information about the author, such as where they work and their role. Websites often have 'About us' sections. Look for these, and if in any doubt, Google the person or organisation to check they are not a social media bot or an astroturf organisation (an organisation that appears to be grassroots but has been set up by a lobby group or business).

Purpose

Think about why the information was created: is to educate, entertain, persuade or to sell something? Does the author or organisation have an obvious agenda? Be alert for indications of bias or advertising. Absolute objectivity is difficult for anyone to achieve, and you may still decide to use the source, but you will be able to gauge where it might fall short of fully validating your point and whether you should look for other sources to fill in gaps.

Accuracy

Accuracy is difficult to judge if you are not already an expert in the area, which is why students are encouraged to use academic and other authoritative sources. If the source isn't academic or authoritative, keep alert for inaccuracies in areas you do know about, or major errors in spelling, grammar and referencing. The latter can be a sign of poor quality control.

You can also spot check one or two facts or follow a reference through and see if it looks legitimate and does support the information it's supposed to.

3.3   Places to search

If you're a student you will have two main places to search: the databases available to you through your tertiary institution's library, and the free internet searched via Google or other search engines. It's tempting to stay with what you know, but challenge yourself to explore the library's databases. You'll learn both about searching and the types of information used in your field, which will pay off both during your study and in the workplace. You may even be able to access these databases, or similar ones, through your employer or public library.

Library databases

The databases available through tertiary institution libraries contain information that is not usually freely available online. Libraries pay subscriptions to allow their users (staff and students) access to this material. Databases may contain books, e-books, journal articles and many other types of information. There are many databases, and not all institutions will provide access to the same ones. Different types of databases that may be available to you include those outlined in Table 3.2.

Table 3.2 Different types of databases that may be available to you

Database type	Use it to find	Examples	Where will I find it?	Advantages
Discovery layers	Almost everything: print and e-books, academic and non-academic articles, reports, access points for journals and databases	Varies by institution	On the library's homepage	Easy to search Almost everything in one place
Journal article databases – multidisciplinary	Academic journal articles Academic book chapters, conference papers, review articles	Scopus Web of Science Google Scholar shares some of these features (see sidebar)	Content may be picked up by the Discovery layer Search title of database in Discovery layer Lists of article databases on library website	Useful if you want to focus on academic sources Can be used to identify important (highly cited) articles Good for finding articles based on a known one Can limit to review articles
Subject specialist databases	Academic and non-academic articles Sometimes books Subject specific types of information – e.g. company reports (business)	Business Source (ProQuest equivalent)	Content will be picked up by the Discovery layer Search title of database in Discovery layer Lists of article databases on library website	Useful if you want only subject relevant material Easier to locate specific formats – e.g. company reports
Specialist databases	These databases focus on a specific type of information or format	Westlaw, Lexis Nexis – legislation, cases Factiva – global news, financial information Passport – market trends, reports and statistics	Search title of database in Discovery layer Lists of databases on library website Subject guides on library website	Content usually not searchable with Discovery layer

The free internet

The internet has revolutionised our relationship with information and the way we communicate with each other. It allows anyone with an internet connection to communicate with huge numbers of people. Organisations can also share information to a wide audience without the costs that would be involved in providing print copies. All of this makes amazing things possible. It can give a voice to marginalised people who often struggle to be heard. It allows creatives to share their work and find an audience.

However, this ease of use and wide reach is also available to extremist and fringe groups, conspiracy theorists, hoaxers and other bad actors. This makes it important to know what you're looking at. If it's a site or organisation that's new to you, consider carefully the issues raised in the 'Evaluation' section, particularly authority, purpose and accuracy.

Not as sinister, but worth remembering, is that search engines build up a personalised view of who we are. For example, from the searches we do and the websites we visit, Google knows what we are interested in and uses this to try and increase the relevance of the sites it retrieves for us. In 2011, internet activist Eli Pariser coined the phrase 'filter bubbles' to convey the blind spots such an approach might eventually result in.

As a student, the most valuable content on the free internet is:

- government information, including regulations, advice, policy and research documents, and statistics
- similar content from NGOs
- news (from reputable organisations)
- company information – e.g. annual reports.

3.4   How to search

When you start higher education, you need to learn new strategies for searching for information: a simple Google search can be unhelpful and misleading. The key steps you need to know are outlined below.

Find your keywords

Most searching that people do is either natural language searching or keyword searching. Natural language searching involves the kinds of sentences or phrases we use in normal speech. Keyword searching cuts out the filler words, leaving only words representing the important concepts. Figure 3.1 gives an example of a natural language search and a key word search.

Natural language searches are often successful when searching the web because search engines like Google consider every word in the web page. They are much less

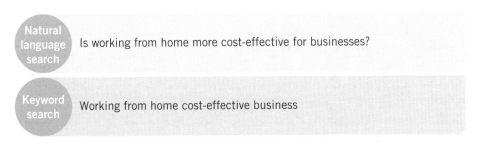

Figure 3.1 Natural language and key word searches

successful in databases because usually the database is only looking for the words in places like the title, the abstract and subject headings.

To identify keywords, remove:

- assignment instruction words – e.g. discuss
- small common words used to create sentences – e.g. in, the
- vague umbrella terms – e.g. issues, effects.

It can take practice to correctly identify the best keywords. If you get very few results, or even none, that can mean you still have too many unnecessary words. For example:

1 The contribution of innovative capital on firm value = innovative capital firm value
2 What are the ethical responsibilities in HR in general? = ethical responsibilities human resources
3 The effect of increased video surveillance on employee behaviour = video surveillance employee behaviour.

The necessity for some of these keywords can be debated – are 'behaviour' and 'responsibilities' necessary in examples 2 and 3? In example 3, could we leave out 'video' and just have 'surveillance'?

Be prepared to experiment! Article databases usually have a feature called 'Search History'. This keeps a temporary record of the searches you've tried, allowing you to rerun earlier searches or revise them.

You may also think of, or see, other useful keywords as you're searching. For example, you might decide you want to focus on theft or trust as aspects of employee behaviour. You can revise your search to *surveillance employee theft*.

You may find that there are other terms for one of your keywords. Working from home is sometimes called telecommuting, so searching 'telecommuting' instead of 'working from home' will bring up different results.

Searching and research is an exploration. Keep your mind open and jot down different keywords and related terms as you find them.

Interrogate your results

Having run your search, what do your results look like? From a quick scan of the first 10, are they on topic? If they aren't, can you identify what's wrong and how you could change your search?

Not enough results (or even none)

First, check for typographical errors (typos) and misspellings. Otherwise, you almost certainly have too many words. Remove any that are not necessary.

You may also have a word that makes your search too narrow. Place names are common culprits, so remove any country names (if appropriate). If it's a noun, see if you can make it more general – for example, *sports* instead of *basketball*, or *retailing* rather than *fashion retailing* (again, if appropriate).

Try using a truncation symbol. A truncation symbol expands your search to different forms of the same word root. The asterisk * is often used for truncation in databases and goes after the last letter that all forms of the word share. For example:

- Manag* = manage, manager, managers, managing, managed, management
- Ethic* = ethic, ethics, ethical.

If you've used double quotation marks for phrase searching (see below), remove them and rerun your search.

Lastly, take out a keyword to make your search broader. Examples are:

- innovative capital ~~firm~~ value
- ethical ~~responsibilities~~ human resources
- ~~video~~ surveillance employee behaviour.

Too many results

With most databases using relevance ranking, don't worry about the total number unless the top 10 aren't relevant. Is there a concept you haven't included in your search? Is there a concept you can usefully include?

If your search includes a phrase, put double quotation marks around it to force the database to search those words as a phrase. Phrase searching works best when a phrase has developed a consistent meaning. It can be too restrictive otherwise. For example:

- Innovative capital = 'innovative capital'
- Working from home = 'working from home'
- Social media = 'social media'.

If your results are relevant but overwhelming, use the database's filters to narrow them down. The most useful are probably:

- date
- limiting to books
- limiting to scholarly articles.

Using database features to manage the process

Databases allow you to 'mark' individual results that interest you on a first scan through your results. This is usually either by a tick box or a folder icon. This acts as a 'shopping cart'. You can then email or save to your computer the results. Items usually only stay in this folder for your current search session (which can time out), so action them before you finish up.

Searching the free internet

When searching for assignments, you could use either natural language or keyword searching. Use the searching advice for databases. You can use double quotations for phrase searching in Google, but not truncation symbols.

Government sites are a source of both regulatory information and research. Restrict your results to government sites by adding your country's government domain:

- 'working from home' site:.govt.nz (New Zealand)
- 'working from home' site:.gov.au (Australia)
- 'working from home' site:.gov (United States).

You can also use this to search for non-commercial sites (site:.org.nz) and to search within specific sites (marketing site:.careers.govt.nz).

You can set date limits on your Google results by looking under 'Tools' just under the search box.

Whether you're searching Google or a library database, contact your library if you're still having difficulty finding useful information. A librarian will be able to make keyword suggestions, identify things that may be blocking your search or recommend a different database. Topics vary widely in how hard they are to search, so feel confident to ask for advice. You'll be a better searcher afterwards.

3.5 Conclusion

Finding information is a skill. Like other skills, you'll get better with practice. Like other skills, learning from an expert will help you enormously. Librarians are the experts at searching and enjoy helping students, so make the most of their expertise. You can do this in various ways – there might be classes in searching as part of your course, there will likely by online help and tutorials on the library website, and you will definitely be able to contact a librarian at your tertiary institution and get advice.

Check your understanding

1. How does searching library databases differ from searching Google or other internet search engines?
2. What are two useful features common to library databases?
3. What strategies would you use if a search retrieved few or no results? What if it retrieved too many results?
4. Can you name two key indicators of a source's reliability or usefulness?

Helpful resources

A way to evaluate different sources using concepts from Te Ao Māori. Rauru Whakarare Evaluation Framework: https://informationliteracyspaces.wordpress.com/rauru-whakarere-evaluation-framework

How to spot fake news. Infographic from the International Federation of Library Associations and Institutions (IFLA): https://www.ifla.org/publications/node/11174

Framework for Information Literacy for Higher Education. Association of College and Research Libraries (ACRL): http://www.ala.org/acrl/standards/ilframework

Information, data and media. An explanation of information literacy (and related literacies!) aimed at students: https://www.westernsydney.edu.au/studysmart/home/digital_literacy/information_literacy

Pariser, E. (2011). Beware online 'filter bubbles'. TED talk, 3 May: https://www.youtube.com/watch?v=B8ofWFx525s

4 Note taking

Note taking is an important skill to acquire if you are taking a business degree or diploma. Of course, it is a skill you'll need once you're working too; for example, you'll have to take notes during meetings (in person and online) and from meeting documents. So it makes sense to hone these skills while you're studying. Good notes serve several purposes. In particular, they help you:

- focus on material you hear or read and make sense of it. If you don't take notes, your mind may wander. Most of us have had the experience of moving our eyes down a page and then realising we've been thinking about something completely different to what we are reading! Take notes to fix your mind on the task.
- reorganise the material for research, writing or exam preparation. When you are preparing an assignment, you need to read multiple resources. By taking notes focused on your assignment question, you can gather all the information you need in one place. And for exam preparation, taking notes helps you to identify key ideas or themes.
- remember important ideas. By rewriting someone else's ideas in your own words, you have to engage with and understand the material. This, in turn, helps you to remember those ideas.

Taking notes also reduces stress (by reducing a lot of reading to a manageable set of notes) and improves your listening and reading skills.

For your study, you need to be able to take notes in many situations, including:

- during lectures, tutorials or meetings – whether these are face to face or online
- from documents such as journal articles, websites and textbooks
- during field trips, work placements or interviews.

In essence, you will need to take notes from oral and written sources, and these two types of sources require different note-taking skills.

4.1 What are good notes?

Good notes, in any situation, have the following attributes:

- They make sense to you. You are the only reader of your notes so they don't need to make sense to anyone else. You can use abbreviations or symbols that are meaningful to you without worrying about whether anyone else can understand them.
- They capture and organise the key ideas you need. In lectures, this means taking down the most important ideas the speaker is trying to convey. For readings, this means taking down only those ideas that are relevant to your task.
- They are brief but well organised, so you can find ideas quickly and easily.

4.2   What skills do I need to take notes?

To take useful notes in a listening or reading situation, you need the following:

- *Concentration.* Train yourself to ignore internal and external distractions. Internal distractions include feelings ('I really don't want to read this difficult text!') and thoughts about other things ('What shall I wear for the party on Friday night'?). External distractions include other people (the person sitting next to you in the lecture theatre who wants to talk or the family member talking on the phone nearby) and other things (the irritating tone of the person speaking, the noise of the air conditioning in the room, the technical quality of the online lecture).
- *Listening and reading skills.* This doesn't just mean the ability to read/hear words. You need to be able to identify main ideas or themes, and differentiate between things that are relevant to what you're trying to learn and those that are minor or distracting details.
- *Synthesising skills.* When you are writing an assignment, you need to be able to bring together ideas from other sources and see how they relate to one another.
- *Organisational skills.* You need a system for filing your notes, and for exam preparation you will have to organise your notes around key themes.

4.3   How do I take notes in a listening situation?

In listening situations, try to ensure the following:

- Avoid distractions. The best place to sit in a lecture theatre is near the front, in the centre of the room. This is where the lecturer focuses their attention, which means that you are more likely to concentrate. Sit away from people who are likely to distract you. If you sit near the speaker, you should be able to hear well and see any visual aids. If you're in an online classroom, try to find a quiet place away from interruptions.
- Have paper and pens that work! Your other option is to take notes directly onto your laptop, but think carefully about how distractible you are. If you are likely to be tempted to check your email or Facebook page during class, take pen and paper instead.
- Head up your paper or word file with *date, course name or number, name of lecturer or tutor taking session.* This helps you find your way around your notes when you are revising. If you are taking notes on your laptop, organise different folders for different courses.
- If you're using paper, number each page consecutively and write on one side of the paper only – it will be easier to read and file later.
- Leave a margin on the left and a gap between sections so you can add material later if you need to.
- Use numbering systems, headings and subheadings, underlining, block letters and highlighting to organise your notes so you can easily identify new points and important ideas.
- Mentally engage with what the speaker is saying. Ask yourself questions: 'What's the key point here?', 'What evidence can you offer for this claim?', 'How does this example

fit the principle?' and so on. In this way, you are an active listener processing what you are hearing.

- During the lecture or tutorial, try to identify the most important ideas presented and write those down. Remember that you're not trying to copy everything down (see the comments below about PowerPoint). In trying to decide what is important enough to note down, make use of all available clues (e.g. how the speaker emphasises different points).

- Use the outlines that the speaker provides on PowerPoint presentations or handouts. These will give an overview of the topic, and they often show major points as headings and subheadings; they may also include unfamiliar vocabulary, names of theorists, important references and significant quotes.

- Listen for verbal clues from the speaker. For example, when you hear 'Three theorists have made significant contributions to our understanding of the product life cycle', prepare to listen for these three theorists and to set out three subheadings in your notes. Again, a verbal clue like 'But there is another perspective on the usefulness of the product life cycle' alerts you to a change in direction.

- Listen for repeated points; a good teacher often makes the points they think are important more than once.

- Listen for changes in volume or in pace of speaking; speakers may raise their voices or slow down for a significant point.

- Don't try to write down everything; listen first to get the overall idea, and then summarise the point in your own words. When you put things into your own words you are mastering the material by understanding the ideas, making recall easier.

- Develop a system of abbreviations for the common words in your field: 'cl' might stand for 'client', for example, or 'mgr' for 'manager'. There are other standard abbreviations you could use as well, such as '&' for 'and', '%' for 'percentage' and so on. Whatever abbreviations you use, you need to understand them when you look at the notes again. You should use the same abbreviation consistently.

- If you don't understand something in class, *ask*. If your teacher allows questions during class, then pluck up the courage to ask a question: the chances are that if you don't understand something, other people are having difficulties too. When lecturers don't allow questions during class, talk to them after class, email them, put a message on an online forum or visit them during office hours. All good teachers welcome student questions, and most will take time to help a student who is genuinely interested.

- Revise your notes in the 48 hours after class, especially if you want to boost your recall of the material. Read through your notes, make sure they are clear, correct any errors and add anything that you think may be important.

- Don't forget to file your notes in an easily accessible way. You need a good system for filing and organising your notes from class.

A note for students studying online: many teachers will upload their face-to-face lectures to be used by an online class. We know, however, that few students watch an online 50-minute lecture right through. This may be because their attention drifts. By taking notes as you watch, you are more likely to stay focused and to work through to the end of the video.

4.4 Beware of PowerPoint!

The biggest mistake students make in taking notes in lectures is simply copying (or taking a photo of) the PowerPoint slides. This is rarely useful. Because you're not putting things into your own words, you're not actually processing the ideas. Also, be aware that different teachers use PowerPoint differently: some put masses of material on PowerPoint slides, which makes copying them difficult, while others may have only main ideas or illustrations on the slides.

Excuse me Dr Loquacious – could you clarify four main points from the last half hour's stream of consciousness?

Always seek clarification

Another problem is that, while you're copying down the slides, you are likely to miss what the lecturer is actually saying, which may be as important as what's written on the slides.

If your lecturer makes the lecture notes available on the course website *before* class, print them out (using the notes option) and take them to class. You can then use them as the basis for your notes and write extra information given by the teacher orally next to the relevant slide.

If your lecturer only makes notes available *after* class, keep track of the slides (e.g. by writing down slide headings or numbers) and take notes about what the lecturer says about each slide. Then, later in the day, transfer your notes to the printed-out slides.

There is another danger with PowerPoint. It is a mistake to think that if you can access the slides, you don't need to attend class. A lecture always contains more information than is carried in slides, and you will miss the verbal cues that indicate whether an idea is important or not.

Furthermore, you may think that you will study the PowerPoint slides carefully, but you probably won't: you'll just print them out, perhaps glance through them for five minutes and file them without really engaging with the material. You certainly won't take the time to reshape the PowerPoint slides into your own words and, thus, internally process them. A lecture (face-to-face or online) is an opportunity to fully engage with these ideas for 50 minutes or more; don't be tempted to take short cuts just because you can access slides written by someone else.

4.5 How do I take notes from reading?

Students often think that note taking from reading material is unnecessary – that as long as they have highlighted key sentences in the text, they will have located the main ideas. This is not a good idea. First, you are very unlikely to truly engage with the material if you just use a highlighter pen. Writing notes, by contrast, means that you have to understand the material to put it into your own words. You will also have higher recall of the material if you transform the ideas into your own words. Another danger that students often fall into, when they have a highlighter pen in their hands, is that they end up highlighting too much. This is not very helpful and means that you will find it harder to locate key ideas when you return to the material.

It is important, therefore, to write notes as you read, either on your computer or on paper. The way you approach the task will depend on your purpose.

A key to effective reading and note taking is to *engage actively with the text*. Don't just read passively. At all times, question what you're reading. Do you agree with what the author is saying? What is the basis of their argument/evidence? How does what this author is saying support or contrast with what other people (e.g. other authors) are saying? Whatever you are reading, don't just take notes about what is written: also include your own commentary or thoughts.

Reading material assigned for class preparation

Sometimes your tutor will ask you to read a chapter of your textbook or some journal articles in preparation for a class discussion (this is called a 'flipped classroom'). In this situation you will need to read the material carefully, but you still need to consider how much detail your tutor wants you to absorb: do they want you to understand the general ideas or do they want you to drill down to the details? You also need to weigh up this task against other tasks (such as writing assignments): how much time do you have available?

If you think your tutor wants you to understand the general ideas within a text, or if you don't have much time, then you need to skim-read. When skim-reading, read and take notes on the following:

- *The abstract* (if there is one). This section of an article is a condensed version of the whole article, so it alerts you to the key ideas, purpose and findings of the article.
- *The introduction*. This identifies the purpose of the chapter or article in more detail than the abstract.
- *Headings and subheadings, figures and graphs*. These indicate the structure of the chapter or article, so you have a clearer idea of how the material is organised.
- *The conclusion*. The conclusion indicates the main findings or ideas of the entire article or chapter, so read this section carefully.
- *First sentences of each paragraph*. Most academic sources are written in deductive paragraphs (for more detail see Appendix B), which means that the main idea of a paragraph is carried in the first sentence of the paragraph. If you need more detail than just an overview without reading everything, then reading the first sentence of

each paragraph will convey more detail. If a paragraph seems particularly interesting or important, you can stop and read it.

Takes notes on each of these sections and you should have summarised the main ideas of the source you're reading.

If you need to read the whole article because your tutor wants you to understand the detail, or if the text is particularly challenging to understand, then a skim-read won't be enough. In this situation, three reading principles are very important:

1 *Skim-read* (as detailed above) first. This will allow you to understand the main ideas and the structure of the article so you can read the detail more easily.

2 *Take notes as you write*. It is hard to pay attention to a detailed or difficult article and you will be more prone to distraction. By writing notes, you will keep your attention focused.

3 *Mark difficult passages*. If you cannot understand a particular part of the material, don't stop: keep reading on and indicate on the article (with a question mark or a vertical line) where the difficult passage is. Often a difficult section is easier to understand when you've read the whole article. When you've finished, go back and see if the difficult passage now makes more sense. If you're still struggling with it, take your time over it, rereading several times, and if you're still confused, talk to your teacher.

TIP

WRITING A SUMMARY

Whether you have done a skim-read or an in-depth read, check your overall understanding by writing a summary of the article or chapter in your own words. This will be a useful reference for you, and it will also be helpful for checking that you understand the material.

Reading for an assignment

If you're reading for an assignment, then the first questions you should ask about any source are: what is the quality of the source and what is it good for? If you're expected to use academic sources for this assignment, does your source have a reference list (if it doesn't, then it's not an academic source)? If you're expected to use up-to-date resources, then you need to be reading recent articles or conference proceedings rather than books (see Chapter 3 for more detail on what different sources are useful for).

The next question you should ask is: will this article/chapter/web resource help me answer my question or (in the case of a report) my objectives? To answer this question, read the following sections of your source:

• abstract
• introduction and conclusion
• headings.

If you decide that this source is worth reading because it is going to be helpful in answering your question or addressing your objectives, then ask whether you need to understand the main ideas or whether you should engage with the detail. Do you need to read the whole article or only a section of it? Make intelligent decisions about how much to read and in how much depth: you're a busy person, so be selective about how to use a particular resource. Once you've decided which parts of a source are important to your task, then read and take notes either by skim-reading or by reading in depth. Use the strategies discussed in the section above.

As soon as you start to take notes from written material for assignment purposes, remember to record important details for future reference. You may want to recheck this source at a later date or include it in your reference list. Noting important details now can save time and worry later. You can record this information in a Word file or on paper, or use referencing software such as EndNote or Mendeley to build up a reference database.

REFERENCING SOFTWARE

TIP

Learning a new referencing software such as EndNote or Mendeley may seem time-consuming at first – but it will save you a great deal of time later on!

The essential details for books will include:
- author
- title and subtitle
- place of publication
- publisher
- year of publication
- ISBN number
- library call number
- source (university library, interloan, etc.)
- chapter and page numbers.
For journal articles, note down the:
- author
- paper title and subtitle
- journal title
- volume number
- page numbers.

For websites, also note down the exact URL for your source (even if it is long!) and the exact date on which you retrieved the information.

For each new page of notes, it is useful to record the source; usually the author's name is sufficient (e.g. 'Fasselbine/2').

4.6   Reorganising your notes

It is often useful to reorganise your notes soon after you've taken them and to restructure them in ways that make more connections for you or that are easier to remember. There are a variety of ways of doing this, and these are discussed below.

Linear system

In a linear system, the notes are subdivided into paragraphs and sections according to main idea and supporting ideas. Use indentations of varying lengths and mark subdivisions by using headings, numbers and other symbols.

1. Note taking
   1.1 Note taking in oral situations
      (i) avoiding distractions
         – being prepared
         – heading up sheets, etc.
   1.2 Note taking from reading
      (i) checking value
         – getting an overview
         – identifying source material, etc.

Princeton method (sometimes called the Cornell method)

In this method, divide your page into three columns (as shown in Figure 4.1). The first is for the heading and main points, the second is for the summary, and the third is useful for reviewing the notes, for noting examples and personal comments, or for an even briefer summary of the summary, etc.

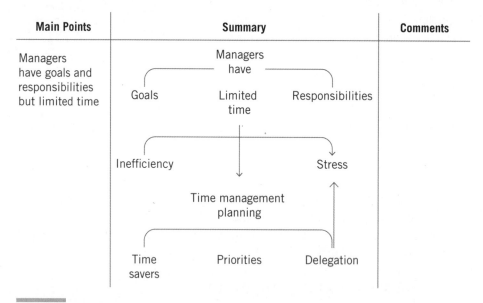

Figure 4.1 Time management

Mind mapping

With mind mapping, begin with the central idea of a topic; add a second level of key ideas deriving from this central idea; and then add a third level of connected notions. Add words that show the association between these levels, as in Figure 4.2.

MIND MAPS

Mind maps are likely to help you to:

» organise your thinking
» see alternative ways of organising the material
» establish connections between key ideas
» remember the material.

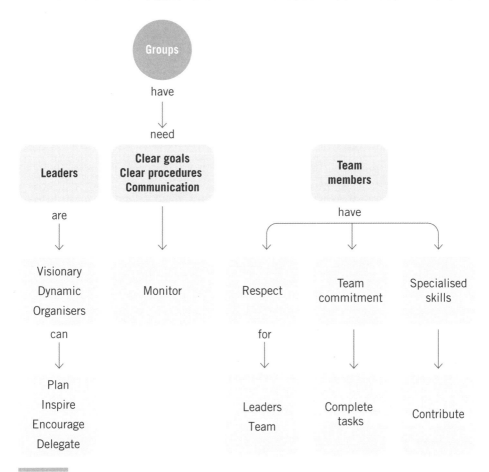

Figure 4.2 An example of a mind map

Be prepared to rearrange your hierarchy according to what you see as important; mental flexibility is a valuable trait. It may be helpful to 'talk' someone else through your map to be sure it makes sense. You may also find it easier to work on A3 paper, or to use an electronic tool, such as Lucidchart, Mindmaster or MindMapper, for very complex mapping.

4.7   Note-taking software

Many commercial and free-source packages are available to help with note taking. If you dislike working by hand, and would like to explore this option, some packages or apps to consider include Evernote, Notability, Zoho Notebook and Notion. These packages all have their advantages and disadvantages, so explore your options. And remember that any electronic package is just a tool: don't get so engrossed in choosing your software that you don't have time for the important tasks of reading and note taking!

Check your understanding

1. Why is writing notes an important skill?
2. What are the dangers of using a highlighter rather than writing notes in your own words?
3. What is meant by the term 'verbal clues'? Next time you're in a lecture, listen for your lecturer's key verbal clues.
4. What problems may you encounter when taking notes from PowerPoint slides?
5. Why is it important to record bibliographical information? Check whether your library runs classes on using referencing software such as EndNote or Mendeley. It may take some time to learn the system, but it will save you time in the future, so it is worth the effort. Some colleges have referencing software available to students at a discounted price.
6. Do you think you would find the linear, Princeton or mind map approach to recording information most helpful? Experiment a little to find the system that works for you.

Helpful resources

A useful page discussing different note taking software and apps. College InfoGeek: https://collegeinfogeek.com/best-note-taking-apps

Tutorials showing how EndNote is used. Don't purchase from this website until you've checked whether the software is available at a student rate from your college: http://www.EndNote.com

Mendeley has a useful set of guides here: https://www.mendeley.com/guides

Useful examples and links related to note taking: http://owll.massey.ac.nz/study-skills/note-taking-methods.htm

A blog post on note-taking designed for tertiary students. College InfoGeek: https://collegeinfogeek.com/how-to-take-notes-in-college

5 Thinking about assessment and group work

In the past, tertiary institutions often relied on three to four types of assessments for undergraduate or pre-degree courses: essays, reports, short-answer questions and examinations. In other words, assessment types at tertiary institutions mirrored the kinds of assessments used in secondary schools.

But as the curriculum has changed over the past two decades, assessment has changed too. Tertiary institutions now set assessments that are specific to a particular discipline or workplace. They have taken seriously feedback from employers that their graduates often don't write with the flexibility that they're looking for, and that graduates in some disciplines need to be able to have skills in composing in a range of media or to conduct practical research. As a tertiary student, you may often find yourself writing traditional assessments, such as essays. But you are also, especially in some disciplines, likely to be asked to write other kinds of assessments, such as blogs, web pages, opinion pieces, microthemes, ethnographies, portfolios, journals and concept maps, or you might be asked to do an individual or group presentation, with slides or multimedia components that are assessed. Sometimes these assessment types will be entirely unfamiliar to you.

This chapter is about what to do when you encounter an assessment type or genre with which you are not familiar. How do you get started? And how do you know if you're on the right track? We also take a look at a particularly challenging type of assessment: the group or team assignment.

5.1 Reading instructions

When a teacher sets an unusual genre of assessment (a genre is a particular form of written task), they have a responsibility to provide students with information about what this involves. You need to read this information carefully. If you still don't understand what is required, you should contact the teacher, but only after you have critically engaged with the course materials and instructions.

A note about exemplars. While you were at school, you may have been provided with exemplars for specific pieces of assessment. While exemplars are sometimes used in higher education, they are not common. You may ask your teacher to provide one if you encounter an unusual assignment genre, but they may not be happy to do so because teachers want you to think and create a piece of writing independently. Sometimes students follow an exemplar too closely, which inhibits independent thinking, and there is a danger of unintended plagiarism.

If your teacher is uncomfortable about providing you with an exemplar, you are, of course, free to search for examples on the internet. But be very careful about using an exemplar. First, make sure it conforms with the assignment instructions. Second, while you may use the same structure as the example you have found and use a similar writing style, take care not to copy or paraphrase any other aspect of the wording: you must write completely in your own words.

Once you have your instructions for the assignment, what types of things do you need to think about next?

5.2 RAFT – the key components of an assignment

One of the best ways to understand what is required of an assignment is referred to as RAFT (Bean, 2011). RAFT stands for: role, audience, format and task. These all work together to determine the structure and style of a piece of writing.

When you find yourself with a piece of assessment in a genre you are not familiar with, you can start by reading the instructions and looking for useful examples. Then you think about role, audience, format and task to clarify your thinking about the writing task. If you're still unclear about what is expected, speak to your tutor or lecturer.

In the following sections, we take a closer look at the elements of RAFT.

5.3 Role

Mostly, role is not an important aspect of thinking about an assignment: when you are writing an essay, for example, you are writing as yourself, a student. But when an assessment has a specific audience, you may be asked to take on a particular role. A client report, for example, might ask you to take on the role of a communications consultant or a marketing specialist. A blog assignment might ask you to take on the role of an expert in taxation law or management theory. Again, part of the challenge of the assessment is for you to write from the position of this particular role. You need to think about the issues outlined in Figure 5.1.

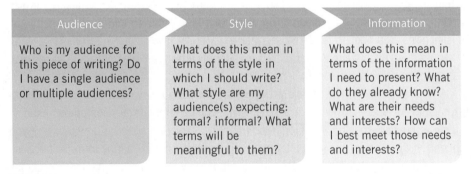

Figure 5.1 Questions to ask yourself when considering your role

5.4 Audience

Your teacher is the person most likely to be reading and marking your assignment. But sometimes writing tasks have a real, or hypothetical, 'audience' – and part of the task is to write for that audience. For example, a blog post or opinion piece is commonly written for a general audience, or for an audience with a specific interest in a topic – so if a teacher has set a blog assessment, part of the challenge of the assessment is to write for a general reader or special interest group. A client-based report is often written for a real or hypothetical business manager or for a range of staff within a company, so you would need to tailor your response to the manager or design a response that meets the needs of different staff within the company. You need to think about the issues outlined in Figure 5.2.

Let's imagine that you've been asked to write a blog post about proposed changes to the Companies Act. If the blog is designed for a general audience, you would include different information and write in quite a different style to a blog written for an audience made up of accountants. For example, a blog for a general audience might explain all key terms and be written in an informal, conversational style (e.g. addressing the reader as 'you'), whereas a blog on the same topic for a group of accountants may not define all key terms (since the audience could be assumed to know them) and might be written in a more formal, third-person style.

A note on essay writing: an essay presents particular challenges in terms of audience since it has no obvious audience (besides the marker, who is an expert in the field). A good way to approach an essay in terms of audience is to imagine you are writing for someone who is intelligent and interested in the question, but who is unfamiliar with the scholarship on the topic.

Once you understand your audience's needs and expectations, you're more prepared for writing the assignment.

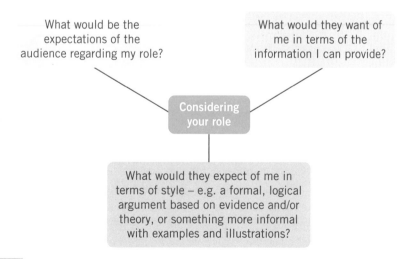

Figure 5.2 Thinking about your audience

5.5   Format

The next issue to consider is the format you've been asked to write in. This is where exemplars or examples can be helpful, although ideally your teacher will have explained something about the format in the assignment instructions. Format relates closely to audience and role, in that the format should meet the needs and expectations of the audience. Some things to think about are outlined in Figure 5.3.

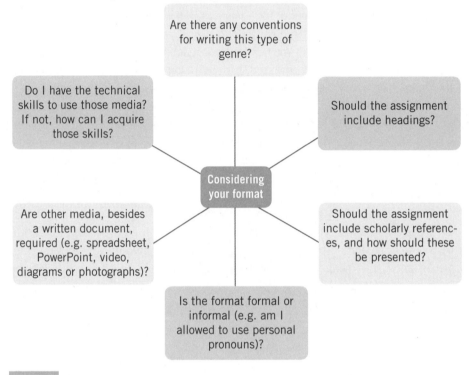

Are there any conventions for writing this type of genre?

Do I have the technical skills to use those media? If not, how can I acquire those skills?

Should the assignment include headings?

Considering your format

Are other media, besides a written document, required (e.g. spreadsheet, PowerPoint, video, diagrams or photographs)?

Should the assignment include scholarly references, and how should these be presented?

Is the format formal or informal (e.g. am I allowed to use personal pronouns)?

Figure 5.3 Questions to think about when considering format

5.6   Task

The next consideration is: what exactly have I been asked to do? You need to be specific about this.

Let's consider the example of a blog assignment asking you to take on the role of an expert in taxation law writing for members of the general public who may be concerned about proposed changes to the Companies Act. But what exactly have you been asked to do? What is your task, your focus? Is your task to allay the fears of the general public about how changes to the Companies Act will affect share prices (and, hence, their retirement savings)? Or is it to simply explain the major changes and their effect on businesses within your country? You can see that these two different tasks (for the same audience, in the same role and the same format) ask you to focus your assignment quite differently. So, make sure you're clear about the exact *focus* of the assessment.

Another way to think about this is to think about *aim*. All forms of writing (or communication more generally) have one of three aims: to inform, to persuade or to entertain. These aims then influence the structure and style of the piece of writing. To go back to our example about the Companies Act: if your task is to allay the fears of the general public about how changes to the Companies Act will affect share prices and, hence, their retirement savings, and you want to persuade your readers to continue their investment in shares, then you will write in a structure and style that will suit this aim – persuasive writing is usually very engaging, and you build up your evidence to make your main point at the end of the document. But if your aim is simply to inform your reader of the changes, then you can start with your main points and then expand on them.

5.7   Review your assignment

When you've finished a draft of your assignment, always take the time to review it. Check the marking rubric or the marking criteria (if they're not provided, ask your teacher for them). Have you answered the question? Have you addressed each part of the assignment? Have you provided everything listed in the rubric or marking criteria? If your answer to any of these questions is 'no', then you should revise your assignment if possible.

5.8   The group assignment

We turn our attention now to an increasingly common form of assessment: the group or team assignment. Learning to work in teams is essential in business, since almost all business careers involve teamwork. While working on these assignments, you will gain essential skills that will stand you in good stead in the workplace.

Acquiring these skills can be very challenging, especially if you are studying at a distance and/or trying to coordinate the work of people with many other commitments. Following are some suggestions to keep your team on track.

At your initial meeting

The first meeting is critical to setting up the project: planning carefully will save you time and trouble further down the track. You will need to schedule at least two to three hours, and everyone in the team needs to be there. These are the essential tasks:

- Appoint a coordinator. It is the role of this person to call meetings, set agenda for meetings and take notes, allocate tasks and enforce deadlines.
- Appoint an editor for the whole assignment. A group assignment needs to read as if it has been written by one person, so you need to allocate this role to a competent writer in your team and give them permission to edit the whole document at the end.
- Decide on how you will communicate with each other (e.g. email, text or a closed Facebook page). Exchange contact details.

Don't use Snapchat to communicate within your team since you want to keep a record of all communication in case there's a problem.

TIP

- Agree on the mark you're aiming for. Problems can emerge in teams when there has been no discussion about the mark you're aiming for, and some people in the team are aiming for As (this is compounded if they're trying get into a limited entry program) while others have a 'Cs make degrees' approach. You need to talk through any differences and come to an agreement.
- Decide how often you will meet (either virtually or in person).
- Choose a platform to write on. When you are working with multiple drafts written by different people, it is easiest to work on an online platform where you can view and edit each other's work, such as Google Drive.
- Consider whether the project is big enough to warrant the use of a project management tool (your institution may provide students with free access to a specific project management tool, or some systems offer free trials).
- Analyse the assignment brief, using RAFT (as outlined earlier in the chapter).
- Once you are sure you all understand the assignment brief, divide the work and allocate initial tasks *with timelines*. Make sure these decisions are recorded and uploaded onto the platform you're working on. When you are allocating tasks, play to people's strengths – for example, if someone is not a strong writer or has poor English language skills, they might best be given a research or technical task so the stronger writers can write and shape the document. Try to be realistic about how much work is involved in each task.

Keeping going and completing the task

The role of the coordinator is to keep everyone on task and meeting deadlines. Further important points are:
- Every meeting should have an agenda to keep everyone focused.
- You should record the main issues discussed and decisions made for every meeting. This is vital: if you come up against problems (plagiarism, people not meeting deadlines), you will have evidence of how you have tried to address these or who is responsible for the work.
- Once everyone's work is submitted to the platform, you need to do some quality control work. Does each piece meet the standard expected? It is unfair to expect the editor to work with substandard work, so don't miss this step.
- After the quality control work is done, the editor (supported by the coordinator) should work on the whole document. It is essential that they are allowed to edit everyone's work to ensure the document as a whole meets the brief and reads smoothly.
- After the first edit, each team member should read and proofread the document.
- The editor should finalise the document and its presentation, and then submit it.

Troubleshooting

Some teams work together smoothly, while other teams can flounder. Here are some things to do if there is a problem:
- If someone is not pulling their weight – for example, they miss multiple deadlines and/ or meetings – contact your tutor or lecturer. Do *not* wait until the assignment is nearly

due: talk to your teacher as soon as you know you have a persistent problem you cannot solve. Since you have taken notes for all meetings, you will have clear evidence of the problem.

- If a team member hands in substandard work or work that does not meet the brief, the coordinator should return it to them with feedback on how to improve the draft.
- If someone tries to take over the work of the whole group, the coordinator should speak to that person and explain that the work must be distributed evenly.
- The 'Alpha Team': some teams made up of very high-achieving individuals can run into trouble when each person thinks they have the best ideas and refuses to listen to others or to take on menial tasks. To work in such a team, you need to understand team role theory (see below).

Understand how teams work

It would help the whole team to understand something about team roles, so that each person values the others' contributions to the task and to the group. It's easy to overvalue the contribution of the leader and the extroverts in a team. But teams also need the quieter team members who get on with the work behind the scenes, those people who do reality-checks by asking difficult questions and others who attend to the details of the task. There is more information about team roles in the 'Helpful resources' section.

Check your understanding

1. What are the potential dangers of using exemplars?
2. How does 'audience' affect writing?
3. What are the three possible aims of a document?
4. Why should you record notes of meetings for group assignments?
5. What strengths do you bring to an assignment-writing team?

Helpful resources

Bean, J. C. (2011). *Engaging ideas: The professor's guide to integrating writing, critical thinking, and active learning in the classroom*. John Wiley & Sons. This book is designed for teachers but provides more detail about RAFT assignments.

Thinking about audience: https://writingcenter.unc.edu/tips-and-tools/audience

The nine Belbin team roles: https://www.belbin.com/about/belbin-team-roles Note: Belbin's work on teams outlines nine team roles. It is not unusual for a single team member to hold more than one team role – so teams of four to six students may (indeed, should) cover all team roles.

Effective team-working skills: https://www.skillsyouneed.com/ips/team-working.html

How to write effective meeting minutes (with templates and samples): https://www.wildapricot.com/articles/how-to-write-meeting-minutes

6 The writing process

Novice writers tend to assume that writing an assignment has two stages: the first draft and the final copy. In fact, writing a major assignment is a *process* that contains many stages. Students should organise their time wisely to allow sufficient time to do justice to each stage in order to achieve high grades. Everyone has their own approach to the writing process; this chapter outlines various stages students may go through while writing an assignment.

6.1 What does the marker want?

Look carefully at the assignment topic and any directions given by the lecturer. Most assignment questions are designed for a specific purpose. Ask the following questions:
- What format am I expected to use?
- Who am I writing to – that is, who is my audience?
- What theoretical issues are relevant here?
- What is the exact practical application of this theory?

A key approach to working out what is required is to consider what question (or questions) is being asked in the assignment. Almost all assignments require you to *answer a question*, but what this question is may sometimes be unclear. For example, consider this topic:

> The attainment of expertise is a simple matter of extensive practice and knowledge accumulation. Discuss.

To find out what the key question is for this topic, you need to rearrange the topic in this way:

> Is the attainment of expertise a simple matter of extensive practice and knowledge accumulation?

Sometimes a topic will lead to multiple questions, like this:

> Compare and contrast models of adaptive and routine expertise. Consider the advantages and disadvantages in a professional field of your choosing.

To answer this topic, you would need to consider a number of questions:

- What is adaptive expertise?
- What is routine expertise?
- How are they similar?
- How are they different?
- What the advantages and disadvantages of routine expertise in, example, the IT field?
- What are the advantages and disadvantages of adaptive expertise in, for example, the IT field?

Once you understand the key question (or questions) guiding your assignment, then you can focus your writing on answering this/these question(s). Identifying the key questions also helps you to focus your information search for your assignment – you should be searching for the different ways in which different authors have answered your question.

Make sure you are fully aware of what is required *before* starting to gather or analyse information; you may waste a lot of time if you do not attend to this first step.

6.2 Gathering information

The nature and amount of information needed will depend on the requirements of the particular assignment. For some assignments the only material needed will be the notes taken from course resources (e.g. readings and activities on the course website and online or face-to-face classes). But most assignments will require extensive library research. For more detail on how to acquire information, see Chapter 3.

If you are using published material, collect this material systematically – this will save a lot of time:

- When consulting a book or journal, write down the basic bibliographical information and keep it in a single file that collects all the bibliographical data for your assignment. Some students may choose to use referencing software such as EndNote or Mendeley and this is highly recommended. You should also write down source details at the top of each page of your notes. This information should include:
  1 author (full name)
  2 title (including subtitle)
  3 publication date
  4 publisher (for books)
  5 volume and issue number (for journals)
  6 page numbers (for books and journals).
- Keep notes for separate topics in separate files or online folders so you can sort the information later.
- If you copy down a quotation, ensure that you write down the quote exactly. Indicate in your notes that this is an exact quote by using quotation marks ('…'), and write down the page number of your quote. If you don't write down the page number, and you later want to use the quote in your assignment, you may have to wade through the whole source to find it again!

- Do not collect unnecessary data. Remember that the purpose of your assignment is to answer your question! Keep your particular question in mind and evaluate the relevance of the material to the topic as you read.

Do not be concerned if you read sources that give different answers to your questions. This is to be expected. On any academic topic, there is a debate. For example, in the earlier question about expertise, there will be some writers who say that extensive practice and knowledge accumulation *are* the key factors to achieving expertise, and some who will say that memory and creativity are more important. And there will be other authors who say that extensive practice and knowledge accumulation are just two of many important factors in the development of expertise. Your job is to weigh up all the different points of view and come to an informed conclusion of your own.

6.3   Generating your own ideas

You may choose to generate your own ideas prior to or after gathering information, or at both times. Either way, do not underestimate your own ideas. Try brainstorming or free-writing – writing down all your thoughts on a topic without censoring them. Talk to anyone – classmates, flatmates, parents, partner – who will listen. You probably know more than you realise about the particular topic, but this knowledge needs to be brought to the surface. Have confidence in your own ideas, thoughts and intelligence.

Read your sources through carefully. And remember to interact with your source. Just because it's been published doesn't mean it's right! Evaluate what you read. Ask yourself on what basis the author is claiming their point of view. Are you convinced by them? Have confidence in your own ability to assess what each author is saying.

6.4   Drafting

The next stage is drafting. From here on, it is extremely important that you keep saving your work. Better still, think about composing on an online platform, such as Google Drive. Far too many students have lost all their work just before their deadline because they didn't save the document as they wrote it. Don't let that be you!

Drafting – writing the first draft of an assignment – is perhaps the most difficult, frustrating and, surprisingly at times, exhilarating part of the writing process.

Allow plenty of time for drafting. You are unlikely to write anything perfectly at first try. You must write and rewrite. Generally, the more drafts, the better the final version.

So, you have a pile of notes, statistics, printouts and a clutter of ideas in your head. How can it all be organised? The following steps may be helpful:

- Find a favourite location in a comfortable (and *quiet*) environment. Assemble your favourite supplies. Make yourself inaccessible (the library, which is full of acquaintances and friends who may lure you into the student cafe, is not a good place for drafting).

- Slowly reread all your notes. Carefully review any outline made to guide the paper. Think carefully about your question(s).
- Set aside your preliminary notes and type the draft as quickly as possible. Imagine you are writing the answer to your question(s) for someone who really needs to be convinced of your answer. Don't stop. If you are writing an assignment that is structured in sections (e.g. a business report or research report), start with the easiest sections. Don't reread your writing. Skip lines if you have blanks.

Make yourself inaccessible

- Don't worry about small mistakes or stylistic issues and don't linger over small problems. Concentrate on developing ideas and working out the structure.
- Although you should take a relaxed approach to drafting, still be careful about your sources. If you quote anything in your draft, indicate in the text that it is a quote and record the source and page number of the source. If you paraphrase material from another source, again record the author and page number. It is very easy to plagiarise by accident, so be fussy about this, even in the earliest draft.

Writer's block

Everyone gets a mental block occasionally – indeed, some of us get them with alarming regularity!

If you just do not know where to start, break the block by using this 'free writing' exercise:

1 Set yourself a reasonable length of time (e.g. 20 minutes).
2 Isolate yourself and remove all distractions (e.g. tell your flatmates/family members you are not to be disturbed. Leave your phone in another room).
3 Write/type up your question at the top of the page.
4 Imagine you are telling a specific person (a parent, partner, friend) everything you know about the answer to this question. Visualise the person.
5 Start writing. Don't evaluate what you're writing, don't try to organise it – just get it down. You can evaluate your ideas and expression later.
6 Finish when the allocated time is up. Take a break and then come back and read what you've written – you should have broken your writer's block and will now be able to work with what you've written.

6.5 Revising

When you have finished the first draft, you should always take a break so that you can come back to your manuscript and see it through fresh, and more detached, eyes: revision (re-vision) literally means to 're-see'. In the revision stage you should focus on the content and structure of the work – again, not on stylistic issues – looking at the wood, not the trees.

Ask yourself the following questions:

- Have I done exactly what was required of me – that is, does the content match the assignment requirements?
- Have I answered the core question directly?
- Do the key ideas stand out clearly?
- Have I supported my key ideas sufficiently – that is, have I provided enough evidence to convince my reader?
- Does the structure of my work highlight my key ideas?
- Would a different structure aid the reader's understanding?
- Have I organised my material clearly in terms of logic, and effectively in terms of impact?

Remember that you are writing for a reader and try to see your work through their eyes. Will it make sense to them? Will your work stand out from all the other assignments your reader will be reading? Read through the paper, writing down the main points in each of the main sections to check the logic of the structure you have used. Reading your work out aloud (or getting someone to read it) may help even more.

Sometimes at the revision stage, you need to pull your draft apart and almost start again with a different structure (though usually with similar content). At other times, you'll find it's just about right and all you need to do is tidy up your draft. If you find you're in the first position, and looking at substantial rewriting, don't despair – you will write much more quickly this time.

6.6 Editing

Editing refers to making changes to sentence structure and replacing words. Your focus should be on readability and style: now is the time to look at the trees rather than the wood! When you edit a document, always start from the big picture and go down to the detail – that way, if you need to restructure a paragraph or section, you don't have to edit for style twice.

You should be using a clear, uncluttered writing style to draw your reader's attention. Make each sentence clear and to the point, conveying its information in as few words as possible.

Check the following:

- Overall: will the reader be able to follow the logic of my argument?
- Paragraphs:
  - Have I discussed just one idea per paragraph?
  - Does each paragraph have a topic sentence?

- Are the paragraphs a reasonable length?
- Have I built effective transitions between paragraphs (which lead the reader to see the relationships between the different ideas)?
- Sentences:
  - Are any sentences too long?
  - Are the sentences complete?
  - Are the sentences different lengths?
  - Are my sentences easy to follow?
- Words:
  - Is the spelling correct? Use a dictionary to check any words you are unsure about.
  - Are slang and casual expressions avoided?
  - Are there any unnecessary padding words that could be cut?
- Punctuation (see Appendix B)
- Gender-neutral language
- Referencing (see Chapter 13)

TIP

EDITING IS PART OF YOUR WORK

While it is fine to ask someone to take a look at your assignment at this stage (e.g. a writing consultant, or someone with good writing/English skills), take care not to let them edit your work for you. It is important that your assignment is **your** work, and editing is part of that work.

6.7 Proofreading and presentation

The final draft should always be proofread and final corrections made. However careful you have been, errors will always creep in. Read the document through carefully for *correctness* – eliminate typographical errors, check the quotes and check the little things, such as page numbers and whether the headings and numbering system follow a consistent format.

Ideally you should ask someone else to do a proofread too. This is not cheating: all good writers ask other people to do a final check of their writing in case they've missed something. Often, when we read our own work, we read what we know *should* be there rather than what *is* there. Another reader will read your work without any prior conceptions and they may pick up something you've missed.

6.8 Submit the assignment on time – and reward yourself

You *deserve* it!

Check your understanding

1. List a number of key things you need to do before you start searching for information.
2. How should you indicate a quotation in your notes? Why is this important?
3. What do you see as the key differences between drafting and editing?
4. Why is revising (between drafting and editing) so important?
5. Think about your own writing process in the past. In the light of this chapter, how could you improve your writing process? Make a note of any changes you could make that would improve your writing process.

Helpful resources

The Purdue OWL (Online Writing Lab) is a good source for student writers:
   http://owl.english.purdue.edu/owl/resource/587/01
A useful diagram of the writing process – click on each key word for more information.
   ABCs of the writing process: http://www.angelfire.com/wi/writingprocess
A useful method for planning the writing process: https://owll.massey.ac.nz/academic-writing/assignment-planning-calculator.php
There are many blogs about academic writing, but one of the best is Academic Writing Success: https://www.academicwritingsuccess.com/academic-writing-blog

As a business studies or commerce student, you will be required to write many reports in the course of your degree or diploma. 'Report' can cover a multitude of different writing tasks in the tertiary context: some tutors will use this term to describe what is really an essay with headings, some will be looking for a formal client-based report, while others will have a research report in mind. It is important, if you are in any doubt, to clarify what kind of report your teacher wants from you.

This chapter focuses on a particular kind of report: the report to a client. You need to be aware that reports for clients can vary in structure depending on the needs of the person who set the task, the context and the style of writing that will suit the audience. This chapter outlines the conventions of writing a report to a client, and the different forms it may take.

THREE KEY QUESTIONS

TIP

Key questions to ask yourself when you are writing a report are:

» Who is the report being written for?
» What are their needs?
» What are their expectations?

You should be flexible when determining the structure of your reports, taking each of these factors into account.

You are likely to encounter two different sorts of reports: case studies and organisational reports.

CASE STUDIES

TIP

In a case study, you are given a written description of an organisational situation (either fictional or based on real life) and asked to analyse the situation according to the theoretical principles taught in a particular course or discipline.

PROFESSIONAL REPORTS

TIP

For a professional report, you will be asked to do your own investigation into a real situation (either one that is given or one that needs to be found). Again, you will usually be asked to focus on a practical problem, but interpret that problem using the theoretical principles of a discipline.

Writing reports gives you practice in applying theoretical concepts to a real-life context. If you are planning a career in an organisational context, it is likely that writing reports will be required. Learning to write a report, therefore, is not just a method by which your teachers evaluate you; it is also part of professional development and a way of learning business principles, integrating them into your critical mind.

Organisations call for reports when they have a difficult decision to make. They therefore require the author to exhibit investigative skills, judgement and the ability to write persuasively. Writing persuasively for a report means that you need to appear to be objective. You are required to produce proof or evidence to support your ideas. It is not enough to recommend a course of action; you need to explain why this is the best solution, what its short- and long-term results will be, and explain the reasons.

Remember above all that a report is a practical project. A report assumes that someone has a problem and they want guidance on how to deal with the problem. If you are writing for a particular person, keep that person in mind at all times. Focus on their needs and recommend a solution that can be implemented. Be specific; avoid generalisations such as 'the organisation needs a flatter organisational structure'. Instead, outline an alternative structure and show how it could be implemented and how it would solve the problems.

7.1   Basic report structure

The basic structure of a report contains six sections that can be arranged in two different ways: deductively and inductively. Deductive reports provide the Conclusions and Recommendations early in the document; inductive reports present Conclusions and Recommendations after the Discussion. Figure 7.1 outlines the basic structure of a report.

Whether an inductive or a deductive style is used will depend on the context. If the report is for a very busy person and/or if the material is not controversial, a deductive style is likely to be used. With a deductive style, the reader will read the 'guts' of the report first, and can

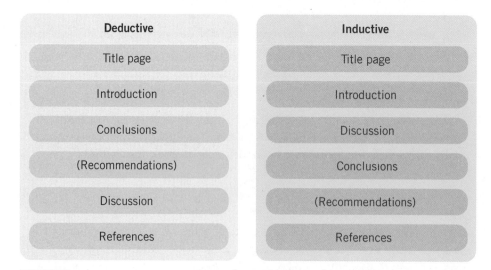

Figure 7.1 Basic report structure

choose to read the Discussion if time permits. An inductive approach might be used if the Conclusions and Recommendations are likely to be controversial or unpopular; an inductive style gives the rationale for decision making before the Conclusions and Recommendations (in the Discussion), so the reader is less likely to simply reject the findings.

7.2   Preliminary and supplementary sections

In some contexts, some or all of the following preliminary and supplementary sections (as outlined in Figure 7.2) may be required.

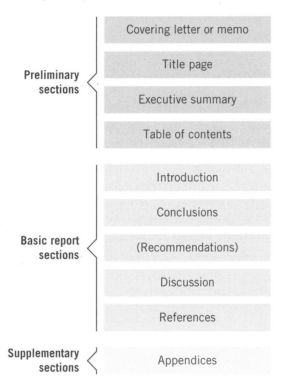

Figure 7.2 A report with all supplementary sections, written in a deductive style

These sections are used when the report may have a range of different readers. For example, if a report is being written for a particular person, a Covering letter or memo can be attached in front of the title page. An Executive summary is designed for the busy senior manager who will not have the time to read the whole report but needs to get a feel for the major findings. The Appendices are designed for the specialist reader who wants more detailed information than the average reader. For example, if the implementation of a new information system is being recommended, then the details of the system, which would be understood by the systems team, would be placed in an Appendix.

It is possible, in a large report, that other preliminary sections will be required (e.g. a list of illustrations or figures, a list of abbreviations or definitions, an acknowledgements page). However, it is unusual to require these of an undergraduate report, so these sections are not discussed in this chapter, except to note that they are usually placed directly after the table of contents.

7.3 Report sections

This section describes the basic content of each section of a business report. There are *conventions* relating to what goes into each section. The purpose of these conventions is to save the reader time. If readers just want to know what the key findings are, for example, they do not have to flick through the whole report; they can turn immediately to the Executive summary or Conclusions. If they want to know the purpose of the report, they can go straight to the Introduction. Use these pages, then, as a guide to mould each section. Be prepared to rewrite some sections until you are confident that the ideas have been conveyed clearly to your reader. If in doubt about the structure of the report, always consult the person who will read or mark it.

Remember that the purpose of a report is not just to complete your analysis. Reports are requested when someone has a particular need for specific information. Communicating your ideas, findings and the interpretation of results from analyses is vitally important. Express the ideas clearly and present them professionally.

Covering note: letter or memo

If the report is for a reader within the same organisation as the writer, a Memo is the appropriate format (Figure 7.3). If the report is written by someone outside the organisation, a Covering letter should be attached (Figure 7.4). The function of the covering note is to pass the report over officially from writer to reader. It reminds the reader(s) of the terms of reference agreed upon for the report, courteously acknowledges any assistance and indicates the writer's willingness to supply more help.

MEMORANDUM

TO: Ms J Evert, Manager,
           South Regional Office
FROM: Mr R Morris
DATE: 19 August 2020
SUBJECT: Report on management and communication problems at the Southland
           office of 'Communicate'.

Please find enclosed an analysis of the Southland branch of 'Communicate', as commissioned by you on 29 June 2020, in response to staff complaints concerning management practices.

I would like to thank the deputy manager, Colin Oates, and the five office staff members involved for their cooperation.

Should you require any further analysis or wish to be provided with any additional information, please do not hesitate to contact me.

Figure 7.3 Format of a Memorandum introducing a report

Communication Consultants
5 Branches Road
DUNEDIN

19 August 2020

'Communicate' South Regional Office
Cabel Street
DUNEDIN

Dear Ms Evert,

Please find enclosed the report concerning management practices at the Southland Branch of 'Communicate' as commissioned by you on 29 June 2020.

I would like to thank the deputy manager, Colin Oates, and the five office staff members for their willingness to discuss issues of concern with me. Should you require any further analysis or wish to be provided with any additional information, please do not hesitate to contact me.

Yours sincerely,

Kaitlin Jones
Consultant

Figure 7.4 Format of a Business letter introducing a report

Aims of a Covering note

The Covering letter or memo should:
- identify the report topic, and scope or extent of investigation
- identify the person who authorised the report and the date of authorisation
- acknowledge any assistance in preparation of the report
- indicate willingness to provide further information.

SUMMARY INFORMATION

TIP

Note that in reports that do not include an Executive summary, you are sometimes expected to summarise the objectives, findings and recommendations in the covering note. If you are not including an Executive summary in your report, check to see whether your teacher would like you to include this information in the covering note.

Title page

The Title page states the report's title. It should be focused and brief, but descriptive enough for the report to be filed appropriately. Position the title by itself about a third of the way down the page, surrounded by white space. Put the date the report was completed under the title. Place your name and the name of the person the report is being submitted to, with the course name and number, in the bottom corner of the page.

Make the title specific and focused. Figure 7.5 shows the correct format of a Title page.

Conflict between senior management
and supervising staff:
Southland Branch Communicate

(19.8.2020)

By: J. Favour
To: Dr I.V. League
Paper: 114.257
         Conflict & Communication

Figure 7.5 Format of a Title page

EXAMPLES OF TITLES

Poor: Conflict at Communicate.
Better: Conflict between senior management and supervising staff: Southland Branch, Communicate.

Executive summary

Executive summaries are often used in reports, especially reports to a wide audience such as a business or company. They reflect the likelihood that the report will have more than one reader, not all of whom are interested in the report's details. A useful summary condenses the essence of the report so that the reader can quickly grasp the report's *aims*, *objectives* and *main findings* (with key recommendations if the report is an action plan).

A common flaw in student summaries is the tendency to describe what the reader would find in the report, rather than to describe the report's highlights. For example, to say 'this report describes production difficulties, supply problems, etc.' does not inform the reader about these difficulties or problems. A better approach would be to name the key production difficulties and supply problems. An example of an effective Executive summary is given in Figure 7.6.

EXECUTIVE SUMMARIES

Note that in an undergraduate assignment, the Executive summary is likely to be no more than half a page. In large industry-based reports, in a professional context, executive summaries may be considerably longer (sometimes running to five or six pages).

TIP

EXECUTIVE SUMMARY

The purpose of this report was to analyse management conflict at the Southland Branch of 'Communicate'. Specific objectives were to identify key problems and offer recommendations to Regional Management.

Problems were located in the organisation's structure, management style and lack of communication channels, especially between the branch manager and the supervisors. The report recommends a major restructuring of the branch, training for key personnel and clarification of job descriptions.

Figure 7.6 Example of an effective Executive summary

Table of contents

If the report is longer than six pages, a Table of contents helps to orientate readers to the scope and emphases in the report. It also gives the page number for the beginning of each section, so the reader can find the section that interests them. The headings of each section and subsection should be identical to those that appear in the report. The logical relationship between the sections should be signalled by numbering, indentation or font size and upper/lower case, or a combination of these methods. See Figure 7.7 for an example of a well-presented Table of contents.

TABLE OF CONTENTS

Figure 7.7 A well-presented Table of contents

Introduction

The Introduction should lead readers from information they already know and share with you, the writer, to information they need to acquire. Begin with a general overview statement that identifies the subject matter of the report and establishes common ground with the readers. Next, provide a short paragraph that establishes the context of the report; this may include a statement concerning the change, problem or issue that has brought about the need for the investigation reported, and why it matters. It is often helpful to present this change, problem or issue in terms of a question that your report will help answer. In some situations it may be useful to state the terms of reference in the Introduction so that the reader knows the specific areas which are to be addressed in the report. Next, define the report's objectives precisely, and in terms that would interest your readers. If you have more than one objective, you may want to indent and list them, so they stand out clearly on the page.

Having given the 'big picture', and then having focused on the issues to be explored in the report, do not keep readers in suspense. The report is written because someone has a question. Summarise very briefly here your answer to the question addressed in the report. Later sections will expand on the conclusions and recommendations in more detail.

Besides introducing the issues the report will discuss, this section should also clarify what readers can expect from the report. Indicate the scope of the report, unless this has been done in a covering letter or memo. 'Scope' means the parameters of the report; for example, you might say 'this report focuses solely on communication issues: it does not look at issues of leadership or organisational structure'. That way the expectations of the reader are clearly managed. If evaluation or judgement is involved, set out the criteria for evaluating alternatives. It is also good practice to identify any limitations of the report – limitations are constraints which you do not have control over. For example, if you have limited access to information, you might write, 'the investigation was limited by only five days' access to the site and the unavailability of one of the senior staff'. Figure 7.8 gives an example of a well-structured Introduction.

WRITING AN INTRODUCTION

TIP

The Introduction should:
» identify the general purpose and context
» describe the change, problem or issue to be reported on
» define the specific objectives for the report
» indicate the overall answer to the query explored in the report
» outline the scope of the report (extent of investigation)
» preview the report structure
» comment on the limitations of the report and any assumptions made.

1. INTRODUCTION

This report was commissioned by Ms J Evert, Manager – South Regional Office. Its purpose is to analyse and advise on how to improve management and communication practices at the Southland branch.

Southland branch is a key branch office for the organisation, supplying essential information to the rest of the company and identifying the needs of regional customers. For this reason, it is essential that the branch runs smoothly. Recently, however, one of the senior managers has noted a lack of motivation at senior management levels. The senior manager also suspects that several young supervisors are causing friction with staff, possibly due to a lack of interpersonal communication skills.

The objectives of this report are:
1. to analyse and make recommendations relating to the organisational structure
2. to analyse and make recommendations on current interpersonal and customer-focused communications.

This report analyses current problems and offers recommendations on how to counter them to improve management and communication practices leading to stability and the continued growth of the Southland branch.
Pivotal issues include the organisational structure and communication and training issues. Restructuring the organisation and instigating new communication and training programs are the keys to addressing these problems.

An assumption is made that the Accountant's position is purely a staff function in line with current business practices.

Figure 7.8 Example of a good Introduction

Conclusions

The Conclusions section of a report summarises the key findings of the report given in the Discussion section. They must be grounded in the *present* situation. They are presented as a list of numbered points that highlight crucial problem areas or issues to be considered by the reader. The conclusions should relate directly to the objectives or terms of reference laid out in the Introduction.

TIP

DIFFERENT CONCLUSIONS

Students often make the mistake of thinking that the Conclusions section of a report is the same as the conclusion of an essay. It is not! It is a list of numbered points identifying the key issues or problems in the situation.

Another problem students have when writing conclusions is that they often want to say what needs to happen. The conclusions should not do this: save those issues for the Recommendations section. Instead, just focus on what is happening *now*. Check your conclusions: if you've used words like 'need, should, must', you've written a recommendation. Rewrite to focus on the present situation. For example, if you've written 'The deputy manager needs to attend a communication course so that he learns effective ways of listening and communicating with staff', you've written a recommendation, not a conclusion. Change it to focus on the present in this way: 'The deputy manager's method of communicating with staff is inappropriate: he does not have strong listening skills, and he is unaware of the need for two-way communication'. Your original statement can then be moved into the Recommendations section. An example of an effective Conclusions section is given in Figure 7.9.

TIP

WRITING CONCLUSIONS

The Conclusions section should:
» identify the major issues relating to the present situation
» be a list of numbered points
» relate specifically to the objectives for the report set out in the Introduction
» be clear-cut and specific
» be arranged so that the major conclusions come first
» be short (full explanation is given in the Discussion section).

Recommendations

While conclusions are grounded in the present situation, the recommendations focus towards the future. Recommendations are the subjective opinions of the writer about the course of action that should be followed. But subjectivity does not mean anything goes. Recommendations should take into account such issues as cost, location and acceptability relative to current policy or practice. Figure 7.10 shows an example of an effective Recommendations section.

2. CONCLUSIONS

The underlying causes of management and communication problems in the branch are as follows:

2.1 Southland's current organisation structure is inefficient. There is an unnecessary layer of management between the branch manager and supervisors.

2.2 Southland is currently experiencing communication difficulties among management, accountant, supervisors and junior staff.

2.3 The branch manager is experiencing difficulties communicating with staff, since he has recently endured a serious personal loss. As a consequence, the whole branch is failing to achieve desired results.

2.4 The supervisors lack training and communication skills. Communicate will soon lose these potentially valuable staff if their manager fails to provide adequate support and supervision

Figure 7.9 Example of an effective Conclusions section

3. RECOMMENDATIONS

To address the current management and communication problems in the branch, the following actions are recommended:

3.1 The Southland branch should be restructured by aligning the accountant's position on the organisational chart as purely a staff function. The unity of command illustrated in Appendix 3 provides for clearly defined lines of command and communication. The manager then overviews and coordinates all of Southland's activities.

3.2 The branch manager needs ongoing professional development: it is recommended that, in the first instance, he attend an appropriate management/communication training program and possibly a grief counselling session.

3.3 The manager, Southland Regional Office, should support the branch manager and provide motivational guidance.

3.4 The branch manager should assist supervisors to develop improved methods of communicating with staff. He should maintain close contact with supervisors and appraise their performance every three months over the next year.

3.5 Supervisors need further professional development: in the first instance, they should attend an appropriate training course on supervision of staff.

3.6 South Regional Office should assist the branch manager in working through revised job descriptions with all staff.

Figure 7.10 Example of an effective Recommendations section

Note that not all reports have recommendations. They are only included in reports that specify a course of action. At least some of them should be immediately actionable.

TIP

Remember to be specific in your recommendations. For example, do not say 'Measures must be put in place to improve communication'. Instead, give specific advice, telling the reader *how* communication can be improved within the organisation.

One way to approach your recommendations is to write in a parallel structure to your conclusions. If you want to write in this way, take each conclusion (each of which will outline a problem or issue) and write a recommendation that matches. So, if your first conclusion is about problems with organisational structure, your first recommendation would explain how to address that issue and propose an alternative structure. Note that this is just *one* way of approaching the writing of conclusions and recommendations.

WRITING RECOMMENDATIONS

TIP

Recommendations should be:

» action-oriented
» feasible
» specific
» related logically to the discussion and conclusions
» numbered (where there are several recommendations)
» arranged in order of importance **or** in a parallel structure to your conclusions
» brief.

Discussion

This is the main body of the report. Normally it will take between two-thirds to three-quarters of the word length. In a student report, this is the most important section as your marker will be most interested in how well you justify your conclusions and recommendations. It should be subdivided into logical units, each with an informative heading and a number. (See '7.4 Presenting your report' for more detail on presentation.)

The Discussion of a report has two main purposes:

1 to explain, in full, the conclusions
2 to justify the recommendations.

The Conclusions and Recommendations sections merely identify the findings and solutions; in the Discussion you explain why certain issues have been identified as problems and why one solution is preferred rather than other possibilities. Show what the long-term effects of the problems will be if the situation remains as is, and what the short-term and long-term benefits accruing from the recommendations will be.

Remember that it is important to back up your claims with evidence from the case or situation. Support the analysis with practical observations and/or with theoretical evidence. Link theory to practical issues. Explain practical effects in terms of appropriate theory. Use theory to give weight to your practical analysis.

It is important to persuade readers of the validity of your stance. If they are going to make a decision on the basis of your analysis, they have to be persuaded that your ideas have value, that they are relevant and practicable. Keep the reader clearly in mind and explain each step of the analysis – take your audience with you.

Present the analysis in a logical, systematic way and divide the material with appropriate headings to facilitate the reader's understanding. If you are using parallel structure with your conclusions and recommendations, then one way to structure your discussion is to take each pair of conclusions and recommendations and write a subsection of your discussion focused on this material (see Figure 7.11). So, if your first conclusion and recommendation are about organisational structure, the first section of your Discussion would be headed 'Organisational structure' and would explain why you came to that conclusion (what is the evidence supporting your analysis) and the justification (e.g. long-term and short-term benefits) for your recommendation.

4. DISCUSSION

4.1 BUSINESS COMMUNICATION

In any organisation, information flow is the life-blood of the business. Josephs (2017) advises that communication is the medium through which action is introduced into the structure of the organisation. Billings (2018) believes that without effective communication businesses fail and relationships wither.

Manager/Accountant

There is little effective management or communication practice between these positions. The supervisory difficulties have surfaced many times, yet no training plan has been developed. The branch manager infers he cannot handle the situation, yet with his vast experience he is in a perfect position to personally coach Harris, Maynard and Cambric to acquire the interpersonal and management skills necessary to work in harmony with their staff. Mace (2014) suggests that the most effective way of providing for growth and development of subordinates is such coaching by line managers.

Manager/Employees

Lack of confidence in both the branch manager and the three supervisors is illustrated by the employees electing not to use upward communication to register their grievances. They preferred to bypass their line supervisors and contact South Regional Office direct.

It is also evident that no facility is in place at Southland branch for staff to freely air any grievances. Sayers' (2008) approach is to have regular meetings so staff know what's happening in the workplace and the executive know early of any problem affecting productivity.

Listening skills

Staff complain that all the supervisors, but Harris in particular, are arrogant, don't listen and snap orders.

Conversations between Harris and his staff should be full two-way communication. However, the evidence suggests that, based on his autocratic management style, he commonly dominates most interactions. Gray and Bell (2005) indicate this leads to managers failing to hear what their subordinates are saying. Effective listening is crucial to effective communication, as it is an understanding between the source and the receiver that must be achieved before they can relate to each other.

Figure 7.11 Subsection of a Discussion section

PARAGRAPH NUMBERING

Note that some styles of report require each paragraph in a discussion section to be numbered (e.g. 4.1.1, 4.1.2). Check with your lecturer to see if they require this style.

A major error in many student reports is that they fail to discuss the recommendations of the report. You must avoid this error. Even if you feel you are being slightly repetitive, you must take the time to explain why you have chosen certain recommendations rather than other possibilities, and what the long- and short-term effects of these recommendations should be.

References

Use the house style recommended by your institution (e.g. Harvard or APA – see Chapter 13) for all assignments. Every report that draws on other people's ideas or findings must have a reference section where all sources are cited in full.

The purpose of the references is to *list all the sources cited in your report.* If sources have been used but not cited, they should not appear in your reference section. If there are sources that have been influential but not cited, they should be listed under the heading 'Bibliography' and should immediately follow the list of references.

Appendices

Material that is complex and/or detailed is collected at the end of the report in the Appendices so as not to distract readers from the main theme.

Appendices may contain supplementary illustrative material that readers may want to refer to after they have read the report, such as questionnaires, letters or pamphlets that illustrate some aspects of the material discussed in the report.

Appendices are also useful places to locate detailed explanations of a model or theoretical approach referred to in the discussion. If some specialist readers – but not *most* readers – would want certain material, it should be placed in an Appendix.

Appendices should always be presented in a professional manner. The material in an Appendix still needs to be organised and presented in a way that is easily understood by the reader. Appendices should always be given a number or letter, and title.

Appendix A:	Proposed Organisational Structure for South Regional Office
Or	
Appendix 1:	Supply Figures 1999–2009

When referring to an Appendix in the body of the report, explain its significance. Do not just add 'Refer to Appendices 1, 3 and 7' to the end of a sentence. Rather, explain to the reader how the Appendix will be of use with a sentence like 'Refer to Appendix A for a more detailed description of this model'.

One of the difficulties students face is determining what material should be placed in an Appendix and what should go in the body of the report (i.e. the Discussion). For example, if you have some figures and graphs that provide more detail about your ideas, should they go in the Discussion or in an Appendix? The best way to approach this is to consider whether the Discussion makes sense without the figure or graph. If it does, then you can probably place it in an Appendix. But if you have to read the figure or graph to understand a point being made in the Discussion section, then that figure should be placed in the Discussion section.

WRITING APPENDICES

TIP

Appendices should be:
» a detailed explanation serving the needs of some specialised readers
» clearly and neatly set out
» numbered (or lettered)
» given a title
» arranged in the order that they are mentioned in the text
» related to the report's objectives and not just 'tacked on'
» listed in the table of contents.

7.4 Presenting your report

The presentation of a report is very important. A well-prepared document looks professional and credible. Clear presentation can prevent misinterpretation of content, and should help the reader understand the material. The following guidelines should be considered a *guide* to presentation rather than directives. Be flexible and consider the needs of the reader and the format of a particular report when deciding on an appropriate presentation.

Page numbering

Each page of an assignment, except the title page, should be numbered, with the number centred at the bottom of the page. Pages preceding the body of a report (e.g. Executive summary, Table of contents) are numbered in Roman numerals. In the body of all assignments, the pages are numbered in Arabic numerals.

Line spacing

Either double spaced or 1.5 spacing should be used for a report.

Each major section should begin on a new page.

Headings and numbering

Major section headings should be capitalised and numbered 1, 2, 3, etc. Subheadings within each section should be upper/lower case and numbered 1.1, 1.2, etc. A report at undergraduate level should require no more than two levels of numbered headings (1.4.3.7 is difficult for the reader to understand within the context of the structure of your work). If minor sections within subsections are needed, do not number the minor headings.

Use a consistent style for headings. All headings should begin at the left margin. Headings at the top levels should be in capitals; only the first letter of each major word should be capitalised for headings at lower levels. Figure 7.12 shows a good example of levels and presentation of headings.

Remember that presentation is an important aid to the reader's understanding and it also helps establish your own professionalism.

1. INTRODUCTION

1.1 BACKGROUND OF THE COMPANY

History
Management Structure

2. DISCUSSION

2.1 BREAKDOWN OF AUTHORITY

Senior Management
Supervisors

Figure 7.12 Levels and presentation of headings

Paragraphs

Do not indent the first line. The text should be flush with the left margin and left-justified. It should begin two blank lines under top-level or second-level headings, and one line under lower-level headings. Leave a single blank line between paragraphs.

Quotations in the text

See Chapter 13 for how quotations should be used in text.

Acronyms

Acronyms are used to abbreviate long titles or clumsy expressions. Examples include NZ for New Zealand or NSW for New South Wales and CEO for Chief Executive Officer.

Acronyms are acceptable as long as they do not detract from the reader's easy understanding of the text. If too many unfamiliar acronyms are used, the reader may need to continually check meanings, which may affect their understanding of, and response to, your text. For this reason, use acronyms cautiously.

With the exception of acronyms that are familiar to most people (e.g. USA), the first time an acronym is presented it should be written out in full and the acronym should be placed in brackets immediately afterwards.

> Ted's Personal Assistant (PA) acted as gatekeeper in this situation.

From then on the acronym can be used without further explanation.
Print acronyms without spaces or stops.

> USA not U S A or U.S.A
> SUWAC not S U W A C or S.U.W.A.C

Numbers

The general rule is to use words to express numbers below 10 and numerals to express numbers 10 and above. However, numbers coming at the beginning of a sentence should be expressed as words.

> Twelve officers remained on the scene and four of these were to remain there throughout the night. The next day, reinforcements of 24 men were brought in, 12 of whom combed the adjacent area.

Visual support

When writing a report, it is important to get your ideas across as clearly as possible, so if a table, graph or list of bullet points will achieve this most effectively, then you should use that visual support. You must, however, be consistent and professional in your presentation of these visual aids. See Appendix C for detail on how to achieve this. If you are using a figure or graph from another source, you must acknowledge that source in the same way as you would any other material (i.e. by providing an in-text reference and an entry in your References list).

TIP

PRESENTATION ISSUES

» Start all new sections (but not subsections) on a new page.
» Only use personal pronouns (I, we, you) in the covering note.
» Use double or 1.5 spacing in your report.
» Use a numbering system to structure your work.
» Present your work professionally, using plenty of white space.
» Use plenty of visual support to convey your ideas clearly.
» Use an extra line space between paragraphs rather than indenting the first line of each paragraph.

Check your understanding

1. Why is report writing such an important skill to master for business students?
2. What are the key questions you must keep uppermost in your mind when writing a report?
3. How does the Conclusions section of a report differ from the conclusion of an essay?
4. What mistake do students often make when writing an Executive summary?
5. List the key differences between an Executive summary and an Introduction section.
6. List two ways of structuring your Conclusions and Recommendations.
7. Why do acronyms sometimes cause problems for readers?

Helpful resources

Massey University's OWLL has a great section on writing a business report: http://owll.massey.ac.nz/assignment-types/business-reports.htm

A good guide to the key principles of report writing. Alan Thompson, Entrepreneurship and Business: http://bestentrepreneur.murdoch.edu.au/Guide_To_Report_Writing.pdf

Useful tips and tricks on report writing. GCF Global: https://edu.gcfglobal.org/en/business-communication/how-to-write-a-powerful-business-report/1

A great video on report writing for business. University of the Sunshine Coast: https://www.youtube.com/watch?v=V8uF1EoIneE

For reports using APA style, a useful source is: https://www.scribbr.com/apa-style/format

8 Essays

Essays are primarily a learning tool – an essay will never be required in a business context. Students are required to write essays as part of internal assessments and in exam situations. This chapter considers essays in general. If you are preparing for exam essays, you should read both this section and Appendix D: Exam skills.

Essays require some very specific skills. They require the student to acquire and assess a range of information in the light of a particular question. This means that you need to distinguish between different sorts of information, evaluate what others have said and then formulate your own ideas in the context of these different perspectives. Finally, your ideas need to be presented in such a way that the reader knows that you understand the debate on a particular topic and can logically present a case for a specific perspective on the topic.

8.1   Essay structure

An essay is a persuasive document. This means you are trying to convince the reader that your position on your topic is the correct one. You achieve this by stating your position (your thesis statement) in the introduction and then justifying this position by marshalling good-quality evidence in a logical fashion. At the end of the essay, you restate your main idea and your reader, having read all the evidence you have provided, and through the logic of what you have said, should be convinced of that main idea. Sometimes an essay is described as 'presenting an argument'. This doesn't mean you're arguing with someone! It means that you have presented a point of view (based on your ideas combined with the ideas of other qualified people) and set out to convince your reader that you are right.

I thought that I would take a creative approach to this essay!

Essays have a remarkably simple structure compared with reports. In English teachers' jargon, the structure of an essay is the statement and logical defence of a thesis statement. Put more simply, this means that an essay states a key point – or series of points – (a thesis statement) in its introduction. The body of the essay then explains these key points: what evidence supports these points? It may also consider why the opposing position(s) is weak: what figures, facts and ideas can be used to defend this perspective? Then, at the end, the essay summarises the main supporting evidence and restates the key point – that is, the thesis statement.

Usually the essay is set out as a single unit without headings; however, some lecturers or markers will prefer headings. The general rule to follow is outlined in Figure 8.1.

Do not use headings in essays unless you have been specifically directed to use them by a teacher. If in doubt, ask your lecturer or tutor.

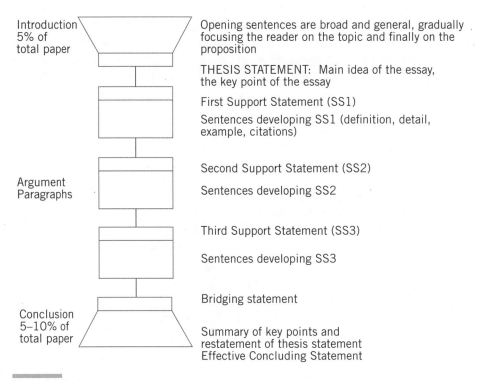

Figure 8.1 Basic essay structure

Introduction

Introductions usually start with broad and general statements about the topic and become gradually more focused until the key points (your thesis statement) are stated at the end of the introduction. Some background information, a question, dilemma or paradox, or an eye-catching quotation might be used at the beginning, but avoid starting with dictionary definitions, a restatement of the topic or the utterly boring 'The purpose of this essay is to prove that …'. Aim to grab the interest of your reader and draw them into the topic.

Remember, your key idea(s) – your thesis statement – should be placed at the end of the introduction. An essay is *not* like a short story – it does not require a surprise ending. The reader wants to know exactly what you are talking about early on, so they can assess the quality of your argument.

TIP

Body

The body of the essay is made up of paragraphs. Each paragraph is a single building block in the construction of your essay and should contain a single idea. The key idea of each paragraph should be situated at the *beginning* of the paragraph (the topic sentence), with the rest of the paragraph supporting, defending and explaining that idea. See Appendix B for more on paragraphing.

Do not forget to consider all the evidence *against* your case. Explain why you have, nevertheless, decided to support *your* proposition.

TIP

Conclusion

The conclusion should summarise the supporting evidence and restate the key point(s) or thesis statement. It is often appropriate to widen the perspective in the final paragraph, showing how your study has implications for further research. However, do not introduce any new ideas at this stage – the conclusion's main purpose is to sum up.

8.2   The essay writing process

There are many ways to approach the writing of an essay. Whatever approach you use, you need to be aware that essay writing is a process with a number of stages. If you try to take shortcuts (e.g. trying to write it all in one sitting) you will not be able to produce good results.

The following is an approach that you may find useful.

Identify the main question(s)

Every essay answers a question or a series of questions: there are no exceptions to this rule. Your first job, then, is to identify the key question or questions that the essay must answer. Here is an example:

> Team role analysis is a vital tool to enable the smooth running of a small business. Discuss.

If we look at this carefully, we can see the key question embedded in it:

> Is team role analysis a vital tool to enable the smooth running of a small business?

Once you have identified the question your essay will answer, then you have a focus for your work, which makes it much easier to write. Sometimes the question is harder to identify or you might locate multiple questions. Consider this example:

> Compare and contrast Belbin's approach to leadership skills with that of Hersey and Blanchard. Give a considered opinion on which approach would be most useful in a situation where a team leader was not able to maintain focus in a team.

Here you would identify a number of different questions to be answered:

> » What are the similarities between Belbin's approach to leadership and Hersey and Blanchard's?
> » What are their differences?
> » Which approach would be most useful in a situation where a team leader is not able to maintain focus in a team?

Once you have identified a number of questions like this, you can use those questions to provide a structure for your essay. In this example, following the introduction, your essay would have three parts: explaining the similarities between the two approaches to leadership; explaining the differences; and then explaining why one approach would be more effective than the other in this specific context.

Identify and define key terms

The next step is to identify and define 'key' terms. This must include any difficult or specialised terms in the topic. For example, in the topic given above, you might need to define 'leadership', and you would need to be able to define Belbin's and Hersey and Blanchard's approaches to leadership.

Another important word that you may need to define to answer the question effectively is 'useful'. Useful can mean many things: what is it going to mean in this situation? Does it, for example, mean to help someone to understand the situation, or to help someone to solve a problem? Watch out for these unobtrusive words that can affect the way you approach the question. Here is another example:

> Standard approaches to planning are not adequate for producing quality. A TQM approach may yield a more successful result.

There are two vital words here that need defining (as well as the obvious words such as TQM and planning). Did you spot them? You would need to define what 'adequate' and 'successful' mean if you are to answer the question effectively.

Read like a detective

Once you've defined your terms and identified your question(s), it's time to do your literature search. But now your search will be focused. Instead of just grasping for anything on your topic, you will be looking for some specific information: the ways in which different authors have answered or addressed your question(s). Staying focused in your searching saves a lot of time. Remember that you are looking to identify the parameters of the debate on your topic.

Remember also to take care with the quality of your sources. For example, if you were writing an essay on whether protein supplements are helpful in strength training, a Google search might throw up a range of websites that are effectively marketing tools for protein supplements. An essay written on the basis of these sources would not be well received. Instead, you need to be looking at peer-reviewed sources that seek to establish the effectiveness of protein supplements. See Chapter 3 for more detail on quality sources.

Read through your material

Read critically through the material you have gathered. You might like to write down each author's key point (i.e. their thesis statement) and consider how they are answering your question and on what basis.

Always consider the source of your material: is it credible? Critical thinking is vital here. There is a lot of false or misleading information out there. Always ask: what is their evidence? Have they collected data? Are they relying on a theory or a series of anecdotes? If so, what do you think about the theory, and do you think the anecdotes are generalisable? Carefully weigh up all the evidence and start to determine what *you* think the answer to your question is, based on the ideas and evidence you have read. What is the basis of your decision? What has convinced you? Remember, you must base your position on weighing up the evidence of others, not on the basis of instinct or prior experience (unless you have been specifically asked about your own experience): in your essay you will have to defend or explain your position.

Form a thesis statement

Once your position (the way you want to answer the question) is clear in your head, you need to write it down in a one- or two-sentence statement. This is your thesis statement. It is useful to have a clear idea of what a thesis statement is.

> A thesis statement is a short but complete answer to the question(s) posed by your essay.

Here is an example from one of the essay topics discussed above. The question was:

> Team role analysis is a vital tool to enable the smooth running of a small business. Discuss.

Now, here is a possible thesis statement:

> Team role analysis can be a vital tool in the smooth running of a small business but its usefulness is rarely recognised and seldom employed. For those who do use team analysis, however, it provides invaluable benefits: a cohesive team who understand each other's strengths and know how to manage one another's weaknesses; an understanding of, and respect for, leadership; and a way of working as a community to achieve a common goal.

As you can see, this thesis statement is not a simple 'yes' or 'no' answer: it is a complete and considered answer, which includes, in a very concise way, a full answer to the question that has been posed. It has two parts: it answers the question and explains (very concisely) why this is the answer.

The thesis statement can also provide a structure for the essay. If you look at the thesis statement above, you will see it contains four key ideas. These four ideas can each become a section of the essay.

TIP

SOME KEY IDEAS ABOUT THESIS STATEMENTS

» There is never one correct thesis statement: a thesis statement expresses your considered answer to the question, based on your reading. What matters to your marker is how well you justify and defend your thesis statement in the body of your essay.

» This thesis statement will be placed at the end of your introduction and then the purpose of your essay will be to defend and explain your thesis statement.

» It is a good idea to write a thesis statement before you start writing your essay. However, sometimes as you are writing your essay, you will see a need to amend or refine your thesis statement.

» Your thesis statement should be restated (in different words) in the conclusion of your essay.

This is how a thesis statement works in an essay: first, it is placed at the end of your introduction, like this (the thesis statement in this introduction is in bold print):

We know that the success of a business often depends on effective team performance. Yet businesses are generally more focused on evaluating individual input. Managers are then often puzzled by why a team fails to work successfully: they brought together a team of highly skilled individuals so why are they not functioning smoothly together?

Team role analysis can be a vital tool in the smooth running of a small business but its usefulness is rarely recognised and seldom employed. For those who do use team analysis, however, it provides invaluable benefits: a cohesive team that understand each other's strengths and know how to manage one another's weaknesses; an understanding of, and respect for, leadership; and a way of working as a community to achieve a common goal.

Then a reworded form of the thesis statement will be placed in the conclusion of the essay, like this (the reworded thesis statement is in bold print):

Clearly, even when teams show scepticism concerning team role theory, or when team analysis leads initially to increased conflict, managers who employ an effective form of team analysis (e.g. Belbin team role theory) with a work or leadership team achieve improved team performance. **Team members are more motivated, more able to tolerate one another's weaknesses, and more likely to acknowledge and utilise individuals' strengths in the interests of an overall goal. Furthermore, team members who understand team theory are likely to demonstrate an understanding of, and respect for, the leadership style of their manager or team leader.** It is therefore in the best interests of managers and business leaders to gain an understanding of how and when to conduct a team analysis, and to encourage their teams to engage with this process, which can increase productivity and motivation. The outcome will be increased work satisfaction and performance, and higher productivity.

Draft your essay

Now you can write a first draft of your essay. It is a good idea to write the introduction first, since you then have your thesis statement right in front of you and it is easier to stay focused on that statement.

Some people prefer to go straight into writing; others like to write their structure first. Know what works best for you and go for it!

Revise your essay

Some people go straight from drafting their assignment to editing it. This is a mistake. First you need to go through a revision process. This is where you ask the big questions about your essay to make sure you have met the brief and done so well. Here are some questions you should ask:

- Have I answered the question?

- Have I structured the essay clearly? Would another structure (or ordering of ideas) work better?
- Have I addressed opposing points of view?
- Will the reader be able to follow my argument (i.e. my defence of my thesis statement)?
- Will they be convinced by what I say and consider that my thesis statement has merit?
    Be prepared to restructure your work if you hesitate over the answering of any of these questions.

Edit your essay

Once you have been through the revision process and are sure you have answered the question(s), and have ensured your structure and argument read clearly, you can start editing. Look at your paragraphing: have you developed just one idea per paragraph? Look at smaller issues like style and sentence structure. Rework anything that isn't clear. Always ask yourself: 'Could I say this more concisely?'

Check your referencing at this stage. Even if you're using referencing software such as EndNote or Mendeley, you still need to check each reference. Go through each citation and ensure it also appears (correctly) in your references list. Make sure any direct quotes have been formatted correctly and that you have provided an appropriate citation in the right format. More detail on how to do this is provided in Chapter 13.

Proofread your essay

Read through the essay carefully, looking for mistakes (in spelling, grammar, punctuation or word choice).

Ask someone else, whose writing skills you trust, to proofread your work – this is good professional practice, but you must remind your proofreader not to edit your text (or you may be plagiarising).

Think critically about your presentation.

When the essay is returned

Don't forget, when you get your essay back from your teacher, to read the feedback carefully. It's easy to just focus on the mark. Remember, your marker may have taken time to explain how your essay could be better. Think through the marker's comments, and consider whether you agree or not, and how you could improve for the next essay. If you don't understand your mark or the comments on your assignment, visit your tutor or lecturer and ask for more detail: remember, it is their job not just to mark your work but also to help you understand your weaknesses or mistakes and how to improve your work for next time.

Check your understanding

1. Do essays contain headings?
2. In your own words, describe what a thesis statement is and where it is placed in an essay.
3. Why do you think the thesis statement is such an important part of an essay?
4. What should the conclusion of an essay always contain?
5. What does it mean to 'read like a detective'?
6. What is the difference between revising and editing?

Helpful resources

Detailed discussion of writing essays: http://owll.massey.ac.nz/assignment-types/essay.php

Extremely helpful perspective on what the reader is looking for and common pitfalls in essay writing. Harvard College Writing Centre: https://writingcenter.fas.harvard.edu/pages/essay-structure

Ariel Bissett has a very helpful series on writing essays on her YouTube channel. All her videos about essay writing are worth watching (and she has a useful video about academic libraries too). This video on the subject of how to write a thesis statement is particularly good: https://www.youtube.com/watch?v=TotaRoYh6OY

Helpful ideas about how to write good paragraphs (which is essential for essay writing). Academic Skills, University of Melbourne: https://www.youtube.com/watch?v=1n15ZkcX5sM

Writing for the web

Publishing content online is an easy copy-and-paste operation; publishing online content that people will actually read is hard, hard work.

Successful writing for the web requires paying attention to the length of what you write, the order in which it is presented, the way it is structured and its voice, while all the time remaining aware of the expectations and abilities of your intended audience.

In addition, you need to prepare your online content in such a way that your readers can scan your page and decide, within 10 to 20 seconds of arrival, that it is worth their time to read it 'properly'.

9.1   Know your purpose; know your audience

Before you start writing your online content, you must address two important issues:
1   What are you trying to achieve?
2   Who is your audience?

Write down your purpose as this will influence the amount and level of information you need to provide. As examples, if your purpose is:

- 'to *inform* consumers about our company's products', you will need to convey the required information as quickly and concisely as possible
- 'to *teach* staff about a new production technique', you will need to provide a clear description of the technique and sufficient background so that the staff understand the reasons and background of the technique
- 'to help people *complete* a task', you need to provide the necessary steps as efficiently and clearly as possible, making sure you don't cloud them with the reasons, rationale or background information relevant to the steps.

You should refer back to your purpose statement regularly once you've started preparing content, just to make sure that you are still on track.

Identifying and writing for your audience is just as important for preparing online content as it is for paper-based writing. You need to know who will read your content and what they expect to gain from doing so. The more clearly you can define your audience – or a typical member of that audience – the easier it will be to tailor your content and present it in a way that is appropriate for their needs, abilities and experience. For example, are you writing for prospective or current customers, for inexperienced or experienced industry operators, young or old – or both?

9.2　Make your last point first

You need to engage your reader as soon as you can. Expecting your reader to invest time to read through background information and supporting arguments before finally reaching your conclusion is not the way to achieve this.

Use the 'inverted pyramid' or 'top down' style of writing: present your conclusion or main point, follow it with the most important supporting information, and end by providing the background.

This approach has the added benefit that your main point is positioned at the top of the page where it is immediately visible to your readers; they do not have to scroll down the page to find it.

9.3　Use the active voice

Arrange your content predominately in active voice. Not only does active voice help your content become reader-friendly, because of its simpler sentence structure, but it also reduces the word count of your sentences (by 10–15%), resulting in shorter paragraphs which, in turn, flows through to improved readability.

In the active voice, the subject of the sentence is placed first:

- This product is helpful for developing project management plans.

In the passive voice, the subject is placed last:

- Project management plans can be developed with the help of this product.

You can see, from this example, how much shorter and more direct the active voice can be.

Active voice is particularly useful in the topic sentence and opening sentences of paragraphs as it clearly announces the topic of the paragraph, and because these are the sentences that your readers will first scan, you are more likely to engage their full attention.

Active voice also assists audience engagement by allowing easy incorporation of the words 'you' and 'your' into the content. Consider these sentences (the first sentence is in passive voice, the other is in active voice):

1　Free access to factsheets and calculators and a monthly newsletter containing useful information about agrichemical use in vineyards can be obtained by subscribing to our service.

2　When you subscribe you get free access to all our factsheets and calculators, you're sent a monthly newsletter and you get useful advice about agrichemical use that you can apply in your own vineyard.

Both sentences relay the same information, but the second sentence achieves it more 'actively' than the first sentence. More importantly, the active voice version puts the main point of the sentence (subscribe) near the beginning of the sentence, where your scanning audience is more likely to find it.

The second sentence is made even more reader-friendly than the first by its use of 'you' and 'your'. These words help you to engage the reader by appearing to 'talk' directly to them (rather than talking at them). In contrast, sentences written in passive voice do not easily lend themselves to this outcome – the outcome is usually turgid and longwinded.

9.4 Use an informative, independent title and more headings

The title of your page, any headings within the text and the introductory sentences will be the first items scanned by readers when they first visit your page. If they cannot find any indication – within 10 to 20 seconds – that the content of the page will help or interest them, then they will leave it. This is particularly true for those people visiting a site with the hope of finding an answer to a very specific question.

Therefore, the title (especially) and subtitles that you use must accurately describe the content of the page at a glance.

You should also pay similar attention to headings and subheadings within your content. These act as signposts for your audience as they scan your page. If done properly, you will find that you insert more headings into online text than you would in its paper-based equivalent.

9.5 Use (a lot) less text

Be prepared to use at least 50% less text than you would use for a paper-based version of your content, while still retaining the meaning. This won't always be easy, and it will take more than a couple of revisions of your content. You will need to remove words or phrases that:

- have been included solely to emphasise or accentuate a point (e.g. the ~~superior~~ design of the pump provides for …; a large crowd ~~of happy well-wishers~~ farewelled the departing ~~Dolphin-class~~ yachts and their ~~excited~~ crews.)
- unnecessarily repeat meaning, are redundant or are just lazy writing (e.g. ~~already~~ existing; ~~basic~~ fundamentals; ~~alternative~~ choices; die from the ~~deadly~~ Ebola virus; the plum's flesh was yellow ~~in colour~~)
- provide unnecessary details or marginally relevant information (e.g. this procedure, ~~which has taken over three years to develop to its current form~~, enables growers to …)
- are unlikely to be understood by your audience (e.g. jargon)
- do not add value to what you have already written
- can be easily replaced by shorter alternatives (e.g. … the ~~vehicle~~ car was seen by a witness; … ~~owing to the fact that~~ because the new system is more efficient …; … the information kiosk is ~~in the vicinity of~~ near the train station).

9.6 Use (a lot) more white space

Long, unbroken blocks of text on a screen create a visual barrier between your readers and your content. Injecting white space into such blocks helps to emphasise what is important in your text and increases readability.

The main tools you have for injecting white space are paragraphs and lists.

Use short paragraphs

You need to create much shorter paragraphs for online text than you do for paper-based text, but you still need to follow the established rule about paragraphs – a paragraph only discusses a single idea. The trick to producing short paragraphs is to focus on a more narrowly defined idea for each paragraph than you would when writing paper-based text.

Sometimes, this strategy will lead you to writing single-sentence paragraphs. Don't be alarmed – such paragraphs are considered part of good practice for web writing (just look at any online news site for confirmation).

How short is short? As a guide, sentences should not have more than about 20 words in them and paragraphs should not contain more than four to five sentences. A reasonable average length for any web page is 300 to 700 words.

Use bullet or numbered lists whenever possible

If your text contains one or more sentences that describe a series of options or products, then break up the sentences into bullet or numbered lists.

Bullet and numbered lists aid the screen readability of your text in much the same way as do short paragraphs by providing white space and making it easier for your audience to scan the page. In addition, they:

* allow you to convey information in a tight space
* provide a degree of order or, particularly if you use a numbered list, an indication of relative importance.

9.7 Use in-text highlighting of key words and phrases

You can, albeit sparingly, highlight keywords and phrases in your text by boldfacing. This technique is particularly useful when you are trying to educate (rather than just inform) your audience. Highlighted words and phrases help your audience see and register the main points of your text.

In-text highlighting often works well in combination with bulleted lists, particularly when the listed items cannot be reduced in length without losing meaning. Consider the text adapted from Bereiter and Scardamalia (1993) in Figure 9.1.

Don't use different font colours, background colours or uppercase letters for highlighting. The former invariably results in text that looks unprofessional; the latter makes the words or phrases more difficult to read. Don't underline words or phrases to highlight them (as is sometimes done in paper-based documents) – underlined text on a web page conventionally signals a link to another page or section in the current page. Don't confuse your audience by introducing another 'use' for underlined text.

Management can foster expertise by creating an 'expert-growing' environment. Competitive environments clearly constitute one such environment, in that they compel the motivated individual to strive beyond their natural capacity and provide models of achievement. An environment which encourages a professional to reinvest in learning (for example, encouraging professionals to stay abreast of current research by reading in their field or to keep up with new technologies) can lead to increased expertise. Organisations can organise work so that it enables professionals to seek out more difficult problems: shaping work with enough flexibility to allow the motivated individual to both shape and pursue increasingly complex problems will help build capacity. Similarly, providing an environment where individuals are enabled to reconceptualise recurring problems in more complex ways may foster expertise. Rather than relying on management to solve problems, learning organisations can enable workers to look at recurring problems in their workplace from new perspectives and engage in creative problem solving.

Word count: 157

Management can foster expertise by creating an 'expert-growing' environment:

- Create a **competitive environment** to compel individuals to strive beyond their natural capacity and provide models of achievement for others.

- Encourage staff to **reinvest in learning**.

- Enable staff to both shape and **pursue increasingly complex problems** through flexible work organisation.

- Enable individuals to reconceptualise and solve recurring problems in their workplace.

Word count: 60

Figure 9.1 In-text highlighting in combination with a bulleted list

Source: Adapted from Bereiter and Scardamalia (1993).

9.8   Use links intelligently

In-text links have been traditionally used to 'move' readers to another web page on the site or to another site completely.

Links have no parallel in a paper-based medium and consequently their recommended 'best practice' is still evolving. They have two components: the way in which they are presented in text, and the outcome that follows being activated (e.g. clicked or hovered over).

In terms of presentation, links should:

- be brief and meaningful, enclosing no more than two to five words
- be informative, even when read in isolation (so never use links like 'Click here')

- explain why they should be clicked (i.e. what's on offer)
- avoid using verb phrases (to avoid giving readers imperative directions).
  See Figure 9.2 for some examples of well-presented links.

Instead of …	Write …
Click here for the market analysis.	The most profitable insecticide was Tokuthion, according to the <u>published market analysis</u>.
To read more about our new widgets which have been modified on the basis of customer feedback, please <u>click here</u>.	Read about <u>our new widgets</u> which have been modified on the basis of customer feedback.
<u>Find out more about next week's conference</u>	Find out more about the <u>conference next week</u>
<u>Click here</u> to read our Annual Report.	Our <u>Annual Report</u> is now available.

Figure 9.2 Examples of well-presented links

In terms of functionality, you can (and should) use in-text links for more than just moving your reader from the current page to another page. JavaScript-driven functionality, for example, uses links to provide access to secondary information without the reader having to leave the page. Short sections of secondary information (e.g. glossary explanations) can be made to appear when a mouse hovers over an appropriately formatted link (Figure 9.3). This approach is less disruptive to reading flow than a pop-up window.

If you use links to move your readers to other pages on your site that contain supplemental information, consider using 'layer' alternatives that keep the reader on the current page and don't disrupt the reading flow. These layer alternatives use links to toggle the secondary information into and out of view within the current page. This is a useful strategy when you anticipate that some of your audience will require more depth of detail than you can provide 'by default'.

With this approach, you will probably need to work closely with your website's developer to ensure that the code necessary to make the techniques work is in place and operational.

You should follow a three-step process when managing significant hazards in your workplace:

1. Take all practicable steps to eliminate the hazard

Reduce the likelihood of harm e.g. provide and require people to wear appropriate personal protective equipment (PPE).

2. If this is not possible, then take all practicable steps to isolate the hazard
3. If this is not possible, then take all practicable steps to minimise the hazard

Figure 9.3 'Tooltips' are a quick and effective means of providing additional information on the page using a link

9.9 Final word

Writing content for the web that works is not easy. Writing great content will test your ability to identify and highlight the most important parts of your message and to arrange those parts on the page in a way that your audience will both see at a glance and understand.

Check your understanding

1. List two important tasks you need to complete before you start writing your web content.
2. What is the best way of organising your content?
3. List five techniques for making your content more readable to your audience.
4. What is an important design aspect concerning the use of links in your content?
5. List three ways in which the sentence and paragraph structure of web content differs from that for paper-based writing.

Helpful resources

A useful collection of resources on web writing by leading web usability consultant Jakob Nielsen: http://www.useit.com/papers/webwriting

A very useful set of examples of good web writing practices and readabililty tools. The 11 golden rule of writing: https://www.jimdo.com/blog/11-golden-rules-of-writing-website-content

A great set of tips, including very useful guidance about writing with screen readers, scanners and skimmers in mind. WebsiteBuilderExpert: https://www.websitebuilderexpert.com/building-websites/writing-for-the-web

Reference

Bereiter, C., & Scardamalia, M. (1993). *Surpassing ourselves*. Open Court.

10 Literature reviews

In the first years of a business qualification, you are unlikely to be asked to produce a literature review. At more advanced levels, however, you may be asked to put together a literature review in the context of:

- a stand-alone study
- a preliminary section of a major research project.

A literature review is a summary of all the key research findings on a particular subject. It will teach you sophisticated information-search skills and the ability to organise material in a comprehensive manner.

A literature review should be extensive; students are expected to incorporate a wide range of quality sources; books and journal articles, reports, government documents, review articles and newspapers may be relevant to some subject areas. The investigation is expected to be thorough. You can expect to spend plenty of time on your library's website; do not hesitate to ask for advice from a librarian on how to do an effective database search.

10.1 The purpose of the literature review

There are four key purposes of the literature review. These are outlined below.

1 Define and limit a problem

It may be that if you are conducting a stand-alone literature review as an assignment, the parameters of the literature review will have been defined for you. But if you are doing a literature review as part of a research project, you may have to define the field yourself. Most research areas are very broad, with hundreds, if not thousands, of studies in the field; your first job, then, is to define a narrow scope for your literature review, one that is directly related to your research question.

2 Place your study in perspective

The purpose of academic research is to extend and add to the current body of knowledge within a particular field. Unless researchers are aware of the work of others, they cannot build upon an established foundation. A literature review allows the researcher to say:

> This is the central debate on my topic and here are the major themes that are emerging. At present, the strongest position on the topic is X. My research will challenge/provide more evidence for the claims of researcher A, G and R.

Sometimes it is appropriate to replicate a previous study, but this should be done intentionally and for a particular purpose. A literature review helps researchers to make informed choices about a research topic within a scholarly context.

3 Select methods and measures

The success or failure of previous investigations can provide useful material when designing a research methodology. You can assess what has worked before (or not worked) in previous contexts and why. You may be alerted to new methodologies and procedures.

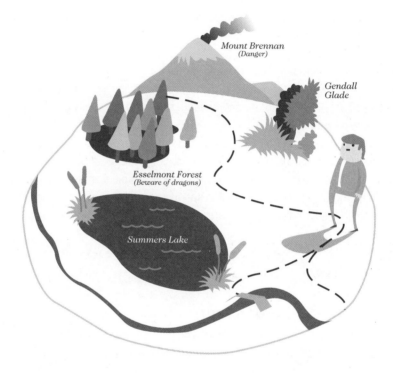

A literature review shows how your work is positioned in relation to the works of others

4 Relate findings to previous knowledge and suggest areas for further research

The findings of your research need to be related back to earlier studies. This 'places' your work and can point to areas that need further investigation.

10.2 Challenges of writing a literature review

A literature review can be a challenging document to write. First of all, you will be dealing with a lot of information from a wide range of sources. A literature review is a comprehensive review of the literature, so unless you are researching in a very new field, you are likely to have a lot of different sources to deal with. If you like to read hard copies, print out as many sources as possible. If you prefer to read online, organise your sources into a folder.

It is important to find a way to organise your sources effectively as this will assist you to locate the information you need quickly and easily. For example, you might initially want to organise sources either by date or alphabetically according to first author.

Second, a literature review is a challenge to write because, unlike an essay, you are not arguing a particular point of view: you are simply presenting the ideas of other people in an organised manner. Remember, though, that you will need to write a summary of the current debate on your topic (which is placed at the end of the literature review), so you are still, in a way, telling a story or making a case for *your* understanding of the current debate. Organise the body of your literature review so that it leads logically to the conclusion you want to make.

Third, because your main idea comes at the end of the literature review, rather than at the beginning (remember, an essay's main idea is placed in the introduction), your paragraph structure becomes very important. You must write in *deductive paragraphs*, where every paragraph has a topic sentence that is placed at the beginning of the paragraph. For more information about deductive paragraphs, see Appendix B.

10.3 Steps in writing a literature review

There are many approaches that can be taken when writing a literature review. This section outlines one approach that you might consider. The diagram in Figure 10.1 illustrates the structure of the literature review suggested here.

1 First of all, turn the topic into a question. For example, if you are writing a literature review about whether the medical profession should engage in advertising, you might turn it into a question like this: 'Should advertising be practised by the medical profession?'

2 Access your library's data bases and search for answers to this question. What you are looking for is an idea of how people have answered this question previously, the scope of the responses and related issues. Collect all your information. Search widely. For a literature review, you need to demonstrate that you are fully aware of the debate on the topic. Ensure that you have accessed all key writing in your field (take care especially to make sure you have located the most up-to-date materials on your topic) and that you are using quality sources (be especially careful with online sources). See Chapter 3 for a discussion of what constitutes a quality source.

3 Now would be a good time to load all your resources into EndNote, Mendeley or whatever referencing tool you're using – that way, nothing will be lost.

4 Many people work effectively with large amounts of screen-based text, but if you're new to working with so much material, you may be best advised to print out all relevant articles. As you read through the material on the topic, see if you can divide it thematically. For example, if you were using the topic discussed above – 'Should advertising be practised by the medical profession?' – you might divide your material into two themes: *What are the critical issues?* and *What are the various views?* Once you've identified these main themes, sort all your material into piles or sub-themes. (Note: you might have more than two themes, or you might divide the material chronologically.)

SPECIFIC OBJECTIVES

TIP

General objective: Should advertising be practised by the medical profession?

1. What are the critical issues concerning advertising in the profession?

   1.1 ethics
   1.2 competition
   1.3 misleading promotions
   1.4 legal status

   ↓

   - legal position would leave doctors legally accountable
   - risk to public would increase

2. What are the various views on advertising by the medical profession?

   2.1 medical council (+ve)
   2.2 medical practitioners (−ve)
   2.3 government (+ve)
   2.4 public (−ve)

   ↓

   - views are equally divided between −ve and +ve
   - those most involved are opposed

↓

- Those who have most to lose are most opposed. Since they are the ones most involved, their rights should be protected.

↓

- No advertising without extensive legislation.

Figure 10.1 Example of a diagram illustrating the structure of the literature review

5   Take notes on all your material. This is very important. If you do this digitally, it will then be easy to divide up further. If you use pen and paper, number or label all your points (e.g. all the notes from researcher A should be labelled 'A', so that when you divide up the material, you know where it has come from). Focus on important material and don't get hung up on detailed results. If you're using your computer or other device for note taking, keep your notes from each theme in a different file, appropriately named. If you're using handwritten notes, put your notes into the appropriate folder. Remember that if you copy any exact quotes from your reading material, you must indicate in your notes that it is a quote (the best way to do this is to put quotation marks around it) and record the page you got the quote from. If you don't do this, you may accidentally plagiarise if you then copy that quote into your writing without acknowledging it.

6   Now focus on each theme, one at a time. Read through your notes, looking for specific trends, ideas or sub-themes that emerge from each theme. For example, in

the topic question used above, if you were focusing on the theme of 'critical issues' you might see specific critical issues being raised by a number of authors: issues around ethics of advertising, the appropriateness (or otherwise) of competition in the medical profession, the implications of misleading promotions on patient health and legal issues. Sort your notes into those themes and then start to define the structure of your literature review by writing a heading for each one. So, for the example we're discussing, your structure so far would look like this:

Introduction to the central question

1. What are the critical issues concerning advertising in the medical profession?
    1.1 Ethics
    1.2 Competition
    1.3 Misleading promotions
    1.4 Legal status
    1.5 Summary of first theme

Go through the same procedure with each theme, sorting your material into sub-themes, and adding to the draft structure of your literature review. The following example shows how, when you have divided your information into themes, you have written the structure of your literature review.

Introduction to the central question

1. What are the critical issues concerning advertising in the medical profession?
    1.1 Ethics
    1.2 Competition
    1.3 Misleading promotions
    1.4 Legal status
    1.5 Summary of first theme
2. Various views
    2.1 Medical council
    2.2 Medical practitioners
    2.3 Government
    2.4 Public
    2.5 Summary of second theme
3. Summary of key ideas in the literature ending with final statement of what seems to be the balance of opinion in the literature to date

---

At the end of this process, you will have produced an overall structure for your literature review, and your sources will be organised according to theme and sub-theme. You can now add one more section: Summary and concluding statement. If your literature review is part of a larger research project, you would add one more short section: a statement of how your research will contribute to this debate.

7   Now that you have the structure for your literature review, you simply need to write up each section. Deal with each section or subsection separately and then add linking statements to lead into each new section. Literature reviews usually have headings, so you can leave your headings in place. Remember to write in deductive paragraphs with clear topic sentences. Don't just write a summary of each source; organise your material according to ideas. Here is an example:

1.3 MISLEADING PROMOTIONS

One of the major concerns regarding advertising medicine is the danger of misleading promotions and the subsequent impact on patient health. Intentionally misleading advertisements are covered by legislation, but advertisements may be written in a way which invites misunderstanding without being demonstrably intentional.

Ambiguity is an example of this problem. Campion (2009), in a study of this issue in North America, showed that advertisements are often written in a way that is not strictly misleading but open to interpretation. This has implications for human health: since in these situations individuals may be self-diagnosing, the ambiguity of advertising, combined with anxiety on the part of the individual concerning a health problem, may lead to use of inappropriate medicine, a worsening of conditions and, in some instances, death (see Allingham, 2017).

A related issue is the presentation of the advertisement. A large, eye-catching slogan may be the only part of the advertisement read by the potential user (Godfrey, 2011). Small print may be more difficult to read and written in language that is difficult for the average lay person to understand (Wimsey and Vane, 2018; Godfrey, 2021). Once again, the health implications are potentially fatal.

A question, therefore, remains: if advertising in the medical profession is to be allowed, what are the legal ramifications?

This example illustrates how a section of a literature review should be written. Under the numbered section heading, the theme is introduced. Then two issues relating to the theme are discussed in separate paragraphs. Note that in each paragraph, the idea is introduced in the topic sentence, and then the authors who have written on the topic are discussed. This is important: your topic sentence must introduce the idea being discussed; only then do you introduce the authors who have worked with this idea. Try to avoid citations in topic sentences, and never use quotations in your topic sentences.

8   When you have written up each theme (e.g. sections 1.1–1.5), write an introduction to that theme.

9   Write a conclusion for each theme.

10 Write a summary for the whole literature review. Remember, you don't have to come up with your own answer to the question (as you would in an essay). But you *do* need to summarise an answer from the literature. For example, 'While the literature on this topic seems very divided, certain key concerns stand out and it is clear that those most affected by advertising by the medical profession are most opposed to this innovation'. What you need to explain is: *what is the story so far?*

11 Write an introduction to the literature review that outlines why we should be interested in this question and what the major themes are.

12 The literature review is sometimes asked for as a stand-alone assignment. But, more commonly, it is asked for as part of a research assignment. When writing the latter, you need to add a paragraph AFTER the summing up paragraph that outlines how the research you are undertaking will add to our understanding of the topic. In this way, the literature review positions your research within a historical and theoretical framework. It defines the boundaries of a relevant scholarly debate and establishes your place within that debate.

13 Check that your headings are appropriate and write new ones if needed.

14 Edit your work, making sure that you have answered your question clearly and that the main themes come across clearly.

A common mistake students make when writing literature reviews is that they just write a series of abstracts, so that each paragraph starts with 'Z says … X says'. This is boring and not, ultimately, very useful: it doesn't help the reader to understand the overall story that the literature reveals. You need to organise the material you have found, as suggested here, so that the reader can see the main themes and issues raised by the question.

A literature review can be challenging to write. But by engaging with the literature on a topic, and identifying key ideas and themes related to that topic, you will deepen your understanding of the field. This is an important step in becoming a scholar.

LITERATURE REVIEW DOS AND DON'TS

TIP

DON'T:

» write a series of abstracts
» start each paragraph with a quote or reference
» leave the reader to make connections
» present the main finding of the review in the introduction.

DO:

» use headings
» organise your material according to themes
» write in deductive paragraphs with clear topic sentences
» introduce sources to support your topic sentences
» present your main findings in the conclusion of the literature review.

Check your understanding

1. What are the main purposes of a literature review?
2. How extensive a search of the literature is required?
3. Do you need to argue a point of view in a literature review?
4. Name one major error some writers make in a literature review.
5. Name one key structuring technique in a literature review.
6. What is the best way to organise your notes?

Helpful resources

Massey University video providing a useful, step-by-step process of how to write a literature review, with an emphasis on critical analysis: https://owll.massey.ac.nz/assignment-types/literature-review.php

An exceptionally good resource on writing a literature review and includes examples, from University of West Florida: https://libguides.uwf.edu/c.php?g=215199&p=1420475

What is literature review? Another useful resource, provided by the Royal Literary Fund: https://www.rlf.org.uk/resources/what-is-a-literature-review

11 Research proposals

11.1 Purpose

Research proposals are most commonly required in advanced courses. However, as tertiary education increasingly moves towards placing the student at the centre of their own learning experience, it is becoming more common to see undergraduate and diploma students asked to produce research proposals and research reports. Research proposals and research reports are also common in a business context, so it is useful for you to learn the required format. Remember that research proposals are, in a sense, persuasive: if you were writing a research proposal in the business world, you would be writing to convince someone that they should fund your research or that your research will provide answers to an important question for the organisation. So, as with a report to a client, you need to keep your reader firmly in mind, follow the conventions of proposal writing, write clearly and concisely, and present your work professionally. Research proposals have benefits for both the reader and the writer, as outlined in Figure 11.1.

Research proposals enable the reader to assess:	Research proposals enable the writer to:
• The rigour of the proposed research methods	• Clarify their purpose
• The value of the research	• Evaluate the literature
• Whether the proposed research will meet its stated aims	• Clarify their methods
• Whether the proposed research can be achieved in the stated timeframe	• Accurately assess the amount of time and money needed for the project
• Whether they want to fund the research or not (if the reader is a funding body)	• Assess the ethical requirements of the research

Figure 11.1 The value of research proposals

11.2 Organisation

A typical research proposal comprises the following sections:
- Title page
- Introduction

- Literature review
- Method
- Ethical considerations
- Budget
- Timetable
- References.

11.3 Title page

The Title page should convey the:
- title of the proposed project
- date of submission
- name of the researcher(s)
- name of the supervisor(s)
- name of the researcher's department
- course number (if appropriate).
  For details on how to lay out a title page, see Chapter 7.

11.4 Introduction

The Introduction of your proposal answers two central questions:
1 What question(s) are you investigating?
2 Why does it matter?

The Introduction generally opens with a discussion of context: from what context does your investigation arise? Is there a gap in our understanding of a particular field (which you are going to investigate)? It is likely that you will give a very brief overview of relevant literature here (perhaps a paragraph or two); a full discussion of the literature is given in the next section.

From here, you introduce your central research question. Next explain why the question matters: why does the question need to be investigated (and funded, if you are writing for a funding body)? Most research, while focusing on a central question, also

A proposal should be persuasive

needs to address subsidiary questions (i.e. questions that arise from the central question). You should outline these questions once you have explained the significance of the central question.

The Introduction, like all of your proposal, needs to be written in a concise manner, without excessive verbiage. Once you have drafted your introduction, step back and read it through again, making sure your reader has enough information to understand what you're going to be investigating and why, and to be convinced about the value of your study.

Sometimes, instead of research questions, your lecturer will ask for a list of objectives: these are a list of things you will achieve through your project. For example, if you were researching the role of creativity in the management of small businesses, your objectives might be to:

- develop an understanding of how managers of small businesses perceive and value creativity
- assess how managers of small businesses use creativity in practice
- develop a model of creativity in managers of small business.

It is common to present objectives or research questions in a list, so they stand out clearly for the reader.

11.5 Literature review

The Literature review answers these questions:
- What does the literature to date say about your topic?
- How have other researchers in the field researched the topic?

Sometimes a full literature review is not required in the research proposal, and the brief overview of the literature in the introduction is enough. But at other times, a full literature review is required, so check the requirements of your lecturer or tutor.

A full discussion of how to write a literature review is provided in Chapter 10, but the key thing to remember is that you have to present a full picture of how your question has been discussed to date. Do not just write a list of abstracts, but make sense of the literature for the reader. What key themes are coming through the literature? Are there any areas of consensus? Are there any key areas of contention? At the end of the Literature review, write a summary that sums up the themes and shows how your research will contribute to the debate on the topic by moving our knowledge forward.

When the reader reads your Literature review, they should have a clear idea of the issues arising in the literature and the contribution you will make. Key stylistic points to remember in writing a literature review are that you should write in clear, deductive paragraphs and that the summary of ideas should come at the end (unlike an essay, where the main ideas are summarised in the thesis statement in the introduction).

11.6 Method

The Method section answers these questions:
- How will you conduct your study?
- Why is this the best way to research your topic?

It is important to describe both your overall methodology (e.g. that you are using action research) and the details of how that methodology will work in your study. For example, if you are using mixed methods as part of your research, you need to describe the overall rationale for a mixed methods study *and* you need to explain how that will work in your research (e.g. 'Mixed methods is most appropriate for this research because…. In this study the mixed methods approach will include a survey and both individual and focus group interviews because….'). Your readers need to be able to evaluate your method, so you should provide enough detail for them to be able to do this. You also need to explain why you are using this method and why it is the best approach to your question.

For some methods, you will need to write this section under specific headings. For example, if you are using a quantitative method, then you are likely to need the following subsections:

- *Procedure*. Provide a description of the research design and any experimental manipulations.
- *Sample*. If you are using human participants, explain who will participate in the study, how many participants there will be and how they will be selected.
- *Instruments*. If you are using a particular instrument (e.g. if you are employing the Belbin Team Role Inventory), describe this instrument and how it will be used.
- *Analysis*. Explain how you will analyse your data – for example, what statistical methods will be used.

If you are using a qualitative research method, you may want to follow the subsection approach listed above, but in other cases you may simply need to develop a rationale for the use of the methodology and a brief description of the development of the method and its specific application in this study. Data collection methods and approaches to analysis should be detailed in full. If your research is based on a particular theory or theoretical approach, this also needs to be discussed in the Method section.

11.7 Ethical considerations

If you are conducting research with human subjects, you will need to consider the ethical requirements of your research. You should talk to your lecturer or tutor about how to address these issues. Do you need to gain approval from a relevant professional body or ethics committee? In your research proposal, you need to outline the ethical issues and how you will address them. Be specific. It's not enough to say, 'The data will be managed according to the ethical guidelines of the organisation'. You need to address specific ethical issues related to the study and how you will manage them – for example, if you need to anonymise the data, how will that be put into practice and how will you store the data?

11.8 Budget

If you are applying for funds for your research, then you need to prepare a budget (if you are not applying for funds, this section can be omitted). Again, you should ask your lecturer or tutor for advice on how detailed this needs to be. Most funding bodies require a detailed breakdown of costs, including even minor items such as postage and stationery, as well as bigger items such as equipment, software, data analysis and travel costs.

For an undergraduate proposal, it is unlikely that this section will be required, as you are unlikely to be conducting research that requires funding. But in the business world, most research does require funding, so it is important to recognise that this might be part of the requirements of your work at some stage in your career.

11.9 Timetable

If your research will take some time, you should provide a detailed breakdown of tasks, to show when the research will be completed. This section is important because, again, it allows the reader to assess the feasibility of your study and whether you have a realistic grasp of what is required. If you are asking for funding, this section also allows the reader to assess whether the project fits with their own agenda and timetable.

There are various ways to structure this section, but a visual representation is often useful. The simplest method is to list task and date for each section of the work in two parallel columns, or in table form. For more complex projects, a Gantt chart or other project management tool may be appropriate.

11.10 References

All studies cited in the background section and the Literature review should be properly referenced in this section, according to appropriate formatting conventions (see Chapter 13).

11.11 Style

The style of a research proposal should be concise and clear. Do not waffle. Keep your reader firmly in mind, and remember that you want to persuade them of the value and validity of what you are proposing. Use deductive paragraphs and simple, uncluttered sentences. If the material would be clearest in visual form (e.g. tables, lists), then don't hesitate to use a visual form.

11.12 Final word

The format and style suggested here apply to student proposals at undergraduate or postgraduate level. In a business context, most funding agencies have specific requirements, which are too various to discuss in this chapter. If you are writing for a funding agency, check to see whether they provide guidelines, and, if they do, follow them precisely. If possible, seek advice from other people who have successfully applied for funding from the particular agency.

Check your understanding

1. Why are students asked to write research proposals?
2. List the key things that must be included in an introduction.
3. What issues must you address to explain your overall methodology?
4. Does your institution have a code of practice for research and/or an ethics committee? Can you find the code of practice or the ethics committee on your institution's website? Bookmark the page.
5. What does it mean to say that a research proposal should in some ways be persuasive? What do you think is the best way to be persuasive in a research proposal?

Helpful resources

A useful resource on how to write a proposal for a funding agency from the University of Michigan: http://www.research.umich.edu/proposals/pwg/pwgcontents.html

Monash University's Research Proposal Guidelines gives a very direct and straightforward description of each section of a research proposal: http://www.education.monash.edu.au/students/current/study-resources/proposalwriting.html

Details on how to write a research proposal and illustrates how to use a Gantt chart to prepare your timetable, by Ketkesone Phrasisombath: http://www.gfmer.ch/Activites_internationales_Fr/Laos/PDF/Basics_writing_research_proposal_Phrasisombath_Laos_2009.pdf

The Massey OWLL provides more detail on writing a proposal here: https://owll.massey.ac.nz/assignment-types/research-proposal-structure.php

12 Research reports

Most students encounter the need to write a research report at graduate level, and occasionally these kinds of reports are required at advanced undergraduate level. The aim of a research report is to report on the findings of a research project to an academic audience and to show how you have advanced the knowledge in your field through your research.

Research reports generally follow a specific format that allows the reader to access information easily. The format presented here is the most common format; however, be aware that if you are writing up research using a qualitative methodology (e.g. ethnography or action research), there may be some variation in how you present your findings.

A research report must have *internal integrity*. This means that your report must establish a research question, investigate that question using an appropriate method and then answer the question (even if it can only do so tentatively). When you are editing your report, you must step back and look at this big picture: have you, in your report, done what you set out to do? Is this clear to your reader?

The style of a research report should be formal, simple and concise (at the editing stage you should be ruthless in cutting out excessive verbiage, and trim your sentences as tightly as you can). Use deductive paragraphs (see Appendix B) wherever possible to ensure your main ideas come across clearly.

12.1 Organisation

The sections required in an academic report, and their order of presentation, are as follows:
- Title page
- Abstract
- List of figures
- List of tables
- List of abbreviations
- Table of contents
- Introduction
- Literature review
- Method
- Results
- Discussion
- Conclusions
- References
- Bibliography
- Appendices.

NOTE: there may be variation in this basic structure. Some sections may not be required (e.g. a list of figures in a qualitative study) and some sections may be collapsed into one (e.g. in some studies the Results and Discussion, or the Discussion and Conclusion, sections are presented together). In a qualitative research project, you may not have a Results section but present your case studies under descriptive headings. Use the generic structure presented here as a guide, but adapt it skilfully to fit your particular project and the needs of your particular audience.

12.2 Title page

The Title page should include the title of the project, the researcher's name and the date of submission (also course number and name and tutor's name if this assignment is a course requirement). Make sure the title is short but accurate: it should be centred a third of the way down the page. If you wish to use graphics on the Title page, keep them simple and professional.

12.3 Abstract

The Abstract is a miniature version of the report as a whole (rather like the Executive summary in a report to a client). An abstract answers the questions outlined in Figure 12.1.

Questions answered by an Abstract

- What did you investigate (and why)?

- How? (For a quantitative study, include compressed details of research design. For a qualitative study, explain the kinds of data collected.)

- What did you find?

- What are the implications of your research?

Figure 12.1 The questions answered by an Abstract

An Abstract is not always needed for a student report, so check with your tutor or supervisor to see if one is required. It is always placed at the beginning of the report.

The Abstract is generally written for a reader who is deciding whether or not the report as a whole is interesting/relevant to his or her research interests. For this reason, it must contain a compressed version of all the information in the report. In other words, it is *not* an introductory section; instead, it contains all key information: why you did the study, what method you used, what you found and the implications of those findings for further research. It must stand alone and make sense to the reader who has not read the whole report.

Because the Abstract is a compressed version of the whole report, it is usually written last (even though it is positioned at the beginning of the report). It can be a challenge to write because so much information needs to be described in very few words. Be prepared to draft the abstract and then edit it many times to achieve the necessary compression. The word length of an abstract should be 150 to 200 words, written as a single paragraph.

12.4 Introduction

The Introduction answers the question around your topic of investigation, your objectives and why they are important, as outlined in Figure 12.2.

Questions answered by an Introduction

- What was the topic of your investigation? OR What was your research question?

- What were your exact objectives? OR What were your subsidiary questions?

- Why does the investigation matter?

Figure 12.2 The questions answered by an Introduction

The Introduction of a research report explains the purpose of the research and why it is important. What will the research contribute to our current understanding of the field? What you need to do in the Introduction is establish in the minds of your readers exactly what you will be investigating and why.

Sometimes it is appropriate to establish the significance of your study by summarising (very briefly) the literature on the topic; for other topics, the significance of the study may relate to a more practical context (e.g. we still don't know why so many small hospitality businesses fail).

Make sure your research question and subsidiary questions (or objectives) stand out to the reader. It is common to list and number these for the purposes of clarity.

At the end of the Introduction, segue into the next section by briefly outlining how you intend to investigate your topic or research question. If you have a hypothesis (i.e. if you expect to find certain results), include this information also.

In terms of style, clarity is again the key issue. Check with your tutor or supervisor as to whether they are comfortable for you to use personal pronouns in the report from this section onwards. For qualitative studies, using personal pronouns is generally acceptable (or even desirable). For most quantitative studies, personal pronouns would be considered inappropriate.

12.5 Literature review

The Literature review answers two main questions about your research question(s): in what ways has it been investigated before and what light do these findings shed on your topic, as outlined in Figure 12.3.

- How has your research question(s) been investigated by others?

- What have findings to date shown about your topic?

Figure 12.3 The questions answered by a Literature review

In other words, the literature establishes the present field of research: the state of play.

In a student research report, the Literature review is written as a separate section in the report.

It is likely that you will have written a Literature review in your research proposal, before you started your research. You may be tempted just to lift your Literature review out of the proposal and put it into the research report, unchanged. Before you do this, though, you should read it through again carefully. It is highly likely that your understanding of the research will have changed since you conducted your research, or you may have altered your research questions slightly for various reasons. This is especially likely if you are doing graduate work and have had a whole year or more to think about your topic. Sometimes people's research questions change slightly in the course of doing the research – in which case, you need to consider whether your literature review from the proposal really still fits perfectly. If either of these is the case, you will need to revise the Literature review you wrote in your research proposal. Many students are very reluctant to engage in this kind of revision, since they are likely to be close to the completion of their project when they return to the Literature review. Whatever you're feeling, try to look at the Literature review objectively, and if some changes or additions are necessary, do put in the work: it will make a difference to the outcome of the final report.

For further information on how to write a literature review, see Chapter 10.

12.6 Method

The Method section answers two questions: *how* did you conduct the study and *why*, as outlined in Figure 12.4.

- How did you conduct your study?

- Why was this the best way to research your topic?

Figure 12.4 The questions answered by a Method section

It is important to describe both your overall methodology (e.g. that you used action research) and the details of how that methodology worked in your study. For example, if you used grounded theory, you need to explain why grounded theory was suited to your research question and then how that method was employed in the study. Your reader needs to be able to evaluate your method, so you should provide enough detail for them to be able to do this. You also need to explain why you used this method and why it was the best approach to your question.

For some methods, you will need to write this section under specific headings. For example, if you used a quantitative method, then you are likely to need the following subsections:

- *Procedure.* Provide a description of the research design and any experimental manipulations.
- *Sample.* If you are using human participants, explain who participated in the study, how many participants were involved and how they were selected.
- *Instruments.* If you used a particular instrument (e.g. the Belbin Team Role Inventory), describe this instrument and how it was used.

If you used a qualitative research method, you need to develop a rationale for the use of the methodology and a brief description of the development of the method and its specific application in this study. Use descriptive headings if appropriate. Data collection methods should be detailed in full.

> Note that the Method section for a research report is written in the past tense. If you are adapting the Method section as described in your research proposal, you need to take care to change the tense.

TIP

As well as being able to evaluate your methods, your reader may be wanting to replicate your study to test it further. For this reason, you must provide enough detail to facilitate this.

Ethical issues are important in any research using human participants, so these should be addressed in the Method section (usually at the end of the section). You need to discuss what ethical concerns needed to be addressed (e.g. protecting the identity, or ensuring the safety, of participants) and how you addressed them. What ethical body oversaw your research? Were any conditions placed on your research by that ethical body? Providing these details assures your reader that your work was conducted with care and thoughtfulness, and according to professional standards.

12.7 Results

The Results section answers only one question:

- What did you find?

Your approach to the Results section will very much depend on the type of research you are conducting. If you are using case studies as part of your research, this is where your case studies would be placed, possibly under descriptive headings, rather than the uninformative 'Results'. Remember that a case study must be reported in sufficient depth and detail here to allow for in-depth discussion in the following section. It is possible to write case studies that combine Results and Discussion, but you should give some consideration to how confidently you can handle a combination of descriptive/narrative style and analytical style; combining the two can be difficult, and you may find it easier to deal with one task at a time.

For a quantitative study, the Results section will have a very predictable structure. You should structure your Results section according to your objectives or research questions, using subheadings. For each subsection, begin with a statement of the main idea or finding and then provide enough data to back up this key idea. Do not discuss the implications of your findings here – save such in-depth analysis for the Discussion section.

Where appropriate, summarise your results in table form, but remember that the same data should not be repeated in several places or several forms. Individual sources or raw data should not be included, except to illustrate samples or in the case of single-subject designs.

Don't be tempted to litter the Results section with tables or graphs about every test you ran. Remember that your aim is to answer your research questions. Therefore, you should make intelligent decisions about what to include to focus your reader on the answers to your questions.

The Results section is generally organised under headings, each section dealing with one question or objective. Use descriptive headings in a logical order (probably following the research questions or objectives as they were listed in the Introduction) to separate your material and to communicate the structure of the section to the reader. Remember that you need to tell a story: make sense of the figures or graphs for your reader. Where you are referring to tables or figures in the text, insert them as closely as possible to the point where they are cited and discussed. See Appendix C for more detail about presenting graphs and tables.

12.8 Discussion

The Discussion section answers this question:
- So what?
  Or, to put it more sedately:
- What are the implications of your findings, in the light of the literature?
  This is where you answer the question posed by your overall project.

The purpose of this section is to examine, interpret, qualify and evaluate the findings – to emphasise any theoretical consequences of the results, to relate the present findings to previous findings, to consider the implications of the findings and to comment on any limitations of the study.

This is the crucial part of the report – and often the most challenging to write! The Discussion section links your Results to your Literature review; it says this is what I found, this is what other people have found – now, what is the connection between those findings? What are the implications? How have I moved the field forward? What more is to be explored?

This section, in a sense, requires new skills of you as the writer. It requires skills of logical thinking, creativity and lateral thinking. You need to see the connection between all the sections of your work and then look beyond the boundaries of your project.

Students often find this section the most difficult to write because you have to link all the other sections of your report together and show how you have contributed to the research debate on your topic. A good way to get started is to copy your research question at the top of the page to remind yourself that this is the question you have to answer now. You should remove the question once you have completed the section, but including this question in the drafting stage will help you focus.

> The purpose of the Discussion section is to give an answer to your research question, in the light of the literature on the topic and your results/findings.

TIP

12.9 Conclusions

The Conclusions section answers the questions that address further implications, how the study might have been better and what other areas might now be investigated, as described in Figure 12.5.

Questions answered by a Conclusion

- And therefore … (a discussion of further implications for the field of study)

- How might the study have been more effective?

- What avenues of research are opened up by the present study?

Figure 12.5 Questions answered by a Conclusion

In a short report you might combine this section with your Discussion, under the heading Discussion/Conclusions. However, if you are writing a longer report, it is a good idea to include this final section as a summary of the report as a whole.

The purpose of this section is to draw your reader's attention to the contribution the study has made to the body of knowledge on your topic; it summarises the main ideas and their implications, and it shows where more research is needed. It should also identify and discuss any limitations of the present study. Some students feel anxious about doing this, but there is no reason for concern. It is natural that, when you look back with more knowledge and understanding of research than you had when you set up the research, you will be able to see things you could have done so much better. Even very experienced researchers do this. It is better for you (rather than others) to point out limitations or errors, and most research does have constraints. Acknowledge limitations and show how new, future research will be able to improve on the findings of the present study.

12.10 References

Any published material that has been cited or quoted in the body of the report must be listed in the references list at the end of the report. This is very important for postgraduate work, as establishing a clear research base is part of your professional training. This is where establishing a habit of using EndNote (or similar software) can be invaluable. Format your references according to the referencing conventions used by your institution or college (see Chapter 13 for more detail on referencing).

12.11 Bibliography

The purpose of this section is to list the source material that provided the background reading. So, if you were influenced in a broad way by a source but did not either quote or paraphrase any of it, then that source should be listed in the Bibliography.

12.12 Final comment

A research report has a lovely logic to it. You pose a problem or question in the Introduction, look at how others have addressed it in the Literature review, propose a method of investigation, report on your investigation and then look at the implications of your findings in the light of other people's work. You need to tell a story, showing how your work contributes to the field of knowledge. It can be a tough discipline to write a research report, but it can also be very satisfying.

Check your understanding

1. Who is a research report usually written for? In what ways does it differ from a report to a client?
2. In your own words, sum up what should be included in an Abstract. Why is it written to contain all this information? What is the most important aspect of an Abstract's style?
3. Why might you have to rewrite your Literature review for the research report?
4. How should the Method section in a research report differ from a Method section for a proposal?
5. How do the Results and Discussion relate to each other?
6. How do the Literature review and Discussion relate to each other?
7. What do you think is meant by the comment 'your report must tell a story'?
8. Where do you discuss the limitations of your study? Why?

Helpful resources

This video from Griffith University provides a clear step-by-step guide to writing a research report: https://www.griffith.edu.au/griffith-health/learning-and-teaching/transition-and-tertiary-preparedness/guide-to-writing-research-reports

Guide2Research provides a detailed understanding of what a methodology is and how to write about it: https://www.guide2research.com/research/how-to-write-research-methodology

13 Referencing

Referencing is a vital part of all academic work. Most assignments require you to show that you have accessed, read and understood a range of quality sources on your topic. You must acknowledge the sources of information that you use in your assignments. In this way, you:

- distinguish between your ideas and someone else's
- show readers the range and quality of your reading
- direct readers to the sources used, if they want further information.

Failure to acknowledge a source of information, or using other people's ideas as your own, is called *plagiarism*, and is a serious form of academic dishonesty. You should check your institution's plagiarism and academic integrity policy, so that you understand just how important this is. For more discussion of this, see Appendix A.

There are a range of referencing tools available for help with referencing, such as EndNote, Mendeley or the referencing tool in Word. These tools enable you to develop a database of sources, so that you can easily insert them into your document and adjust them to the correct style of referencing. This is especially useful if you are working in a field that uses a range of referencing styles. For example, if management papers require you to use APA and communications require you to use Chicago referencing styles, then the referencing tool can adjust your references from one form to the other at the press of a key. Buying the software is a worthwhile financial outlay (and your institution may be able to provide you with the software for a discounted price, or even for free), and learning to use it is an even better investment. It may take a little time to set up, but you'll be glad you did so, especially when you watch your fellow students worrying over the details of referencing conventions!

Even when you're using a referencing tool, you still need to understand the details of the referencing style you're using, so that you can check the reference list when you're fine-tuning your document. Accuracy and attention to detail are important in referencing. Your tutors or lecturers will expect you to be precise in your use of referencing conventions. This means that you must get the details exactly right, down to the last piece of punctuation. At first you may find this frustrating and unnecessary. But it's all a matter of being professional and ensuring your document looks the part. If your referencing is inconsistent, then your document will look unprofessional. In the end, you will find that referencing becomes second nature, and after you've used one style consistently, it becomes familiar and easy to use.

There are many different systems for presenting the ideas of other sources – that is, referencing. The most commonly used styles in business are APA, Chicago, Harvard and MLA. Most colleges, universities or departments will specify which style you should use, so you need to check this before you submit your first assignment. In this textbook, we use the formatting conventions of the American Psychological Association (APA) for setting out references. Some of these conventions are listed below. For more detail on APA referencing, refer to the *Publication Manual of the American Psychological Association* (7th ed.). If your institution or department uses a different set of conventions, there are some websites that may help you set out your references according to the required style.

13.1 Referencing styles

MLA conventions (8th edition)

- MLA Formatting and Style Guide (Purdue University): https://owl.purdue.edu/owl/research_and_citation/mla_style/mla_formatting_and_style_guide/mla_formatting_and_style_guide.html
- MLA Interactive: https://owll.massey.ac.nz/referencing/mla-interactive.php
- Modern Language Association (MLA) Style Guide (Monash University): https://guides.lib.monash.edu/citing-referencing/mla8

 TIP Note that MLA, unlike other referencing systems, includes first names as well as family names in the reference list, so make sure you record that information.

Chicago conventions

- Chicago Interactive: https://owll.massey.ac.nz/referencing/chicago-interactive.php
- Chicago Referencing Guide (Murdoch University): https://libguides.murdoch.edu.au/Chicago
- Chicago Style (Massey University): http://owll.massey.ac.nz/aw_referencing_ch_2.html
- Chicago Style Citation Quick Guide: https://www.chicagomanualofstyle.org/tools_citationguide.html

A complication of the Chicago system is that it incorporates two kinds of system: a footnoting method that is similar to MLA and a name–date method that is very like the Harvard or APA system. If you've been advised to use the Chicago system of referencing, check which of these two systems is required.

Harvard conventions

- Free Harvard Citation Generator: https://www.citethisforme.com/citation-generator/harvard
- Harvard (Author-Date Style) (Macquarie University): https://libguides.mq.edu.au/referencing/Harvard
- Harvard Style (Massey University): https://owll.massey.ac.nz/referencing/harvard-style.php

Most of this chapter focuses on how to use APA conventions to reference secondary sources. Because of the huge variety of information sources, it is not possible to cover all types of sources in this brief introduction. Instead we have focused on the most common types of sources and provided websites with more detailed information and support within and at the end of the chapter.

TIP

13.2 Acknowledging sources

The APA style of referencing uses inline acknowledgement of sources rather than footnotes or endnotes. This means that sources need to be acknowledged in the ways listed below.

How do I acknowledge an idea that I have expressed in my own words?

Sometimes someone else's ideas, concepts or figures, but not that person's exact words, may be included in your work. This is called *citing* or *paraphrasing* (as opposed to quoting, when you use someone's exact words) and it is an appropriate approach to using sources, as long as you acknowledge the source. In this situation, the source must be acknowledged by putting the author's last name and the date when the work was published in brackets at the end of the sentence.

> Management consultants usually see the formulation of a strategic plan as an essential step for all organisations (Hutton, 2018).
> Many entrepreneurs see educational qualifications as irrelevant (Hutton, 2018; O'Hagan, 2020).

Note that in the second example above, where two sources are cited, each one is separated with a semicolon, and they are listed in alphabetical order.

TIP

Another approach to this is to include the surname of the author within your sentence with the date in brackets:

> As Hutton (2018) suggests, entrepreneurs see educational qualifications as irrelevant.

It is not necessary to include a page number for a citation, but if you are referring to material on a specific page of the text, it may be helpful to include the page number to help any reader who would like to follow up the reference.

How do I include a short quotation in my work?

If the referenced author's own words are being used, place the quotation in quotation marks and include a page number at the end of the reference.

> For many New Zealanders, this country is no longer an agricultural nation. New Zealand has grown, diversified and bounced back again, determined never again to be reliant on a single industry and market. 'We have come of age, internationally' (Lowe, 2020, p. 64).

TIP Note that when the quotation ends a sentence, the full stop comes *after* the information in brackets.

How do I include a longer quotation in my work?

If a direct quotation that is longer than 40 words is being used, the quotation should be indented five spaces and quotation marks omitted. The reference should be acknowledged in the same way as the shorter quotation above. However, the in-text information is provided *after* the full stop.

> Within management theory there have been many changes and developments. One researcher – Lance Gray – has identified equity and diversity as key factors for management success:
>
> > Management of equity issues is a vital factor in determining managerial success in the 21st Century. A successful manager establishes an equity policy throughout the organisation, including diversity milestones, unconscious bias and diversity training, and pro-active hiring practices to address gender and ethnicity diversity within the organisation. It is essential that the workplace reflects, and harnesses the strengths, of our diverse national community. (2019, p. 6)
>
> Such a perspective has support from many other theorists in the area ...

How do I reference an author who is quoted in a book or journal I am reading?

If you wish to use a quotation or cite an idea that is quoted or cited by another author, then both sources should be acknowledged in the text.

> Although much has been written about the negative impact of stress, 'nevertheless, stress can contribute to performance' (Bourne, 2015, p. 33, as cited in Gallavin, 2021, p. 16).

> Although many authors have emphasised the way in which stress can impact negatively on performance, Bourne (2015, as cited in Gallavin, 2021) emphasises its positive aspects.

The reference list, at the end of the assignment, should list only Gallavin, *not* Bourne.

How do I reference a source if I have already used the author's name in the sentence?

Sometimes an author may be directly referred to within the assignment.

> » Tootell (1994) was the first to maintain that …
> » Planning is the first essential step according to Lambert (2020).
> » Researchers in the field (Lambert, 2020; Tootell, 1994) indicate that …
> » She stated that 'the management cycle has four key elements' (Tootell, 1994, p. 16) but did not rank those four factors.

How do I reference a work with many authors?

If a work has two authors, both names should be cited. Note that if the inline citation includes the authors in the parentheses, the names should be linked by an ampersand (&), but if the names are listed in the text, they should be joined by 'and'.

> In their seminal work (Emerson & MacKay, 2011), the authors maintain that …
> Emerson and MacKay (2011), in their seminal work on the subject, argue that …

If the work has three or more authors, only list the first name and then add et al. (meaning 'and others').

> Shaw et al. (2019) also found …

How do I reference a letter, email or interview?

Anything that isn't accessible to other people (i.e. not published in any way) is called a *personal communication*. It is not included in the reference list but should be cited in the text. Give initials of the communicator and an exact date.

> E. C. MacKay (personal communication, December 9, 2021) suggests that …

How do I reference something with no author?

If you are referring to something that has no acknowledged author, such as a web page, then place the first few words of the title in the author position. If you are using the title of a book or report, you italicise the title. If you're citing the title of an article, chapter, newspaper article or web page, use quotation marks. You should capitalise all the important words in titles used in an in-text citation.

> Citing a report with no author: This report (*Management Student Success in the 21st Century*, 2020) outlines the success factors for ....
>
> Citing a newspaper article with no author: The lead story, 'Greenback Plummets' (2021), outlines the reasons why ...

Most legal material is cited in text in this way, but details of how specific types of legal material should be formatted in the text may be found in the *Publication Manual of the American Psychological Association (APA)* (7th ed.). The following website is also helpful: https://owl.purdue.edu/owl/research_and_citation/apa_style/apa_formatting_and_style_guide/apa_legal%20references%20.html

How do I quote something with no page numbers?

Most electronic sources do not have page numbers. Instead, you need to provide a way for the reader to access the source of your quotation easily. This might mean providing details of paragraph number, and heading or section name – or both.

> According to Carusi (2020, Feminist Perspectives on Management section, para. 4) ...

13.3 What is a reference list?

A reference list is a list of the full bibliographical details of all the material quoted or cited in your assignment. Every assignment written must have a reference list. It should be started on a new page and be headed 'References'.

In listing the references at the end of the document, one style guide should be followed consistently. We recommend that you use the style favoured by your institution or department. Here we provide details of APA referencing conventions, taken from the APA Style Manual (7th ed.).

All items must be listed in alphabetical order, according to the surname of the first author.

How do I list a book according to APA style?

Put the author's family name first, spelled out in full, with initials only for first and second names. Give the date of publication in brackets. Next is the title, followed by the publisher.

If there is a DOI, include that too. Note that, on the reference page, only the first letter of the first word of the title and subtitle is capitalised. Title and subtitle should be italicised. The title is followed by a full stop, as is the publisher. Punctuation details are expected to be accurate (see Figure 13.1).

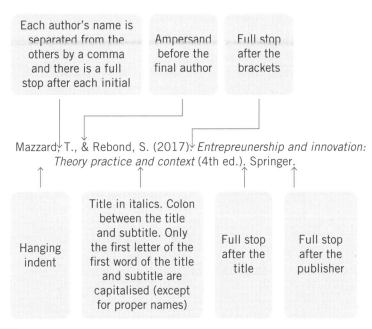

Figure 13.1 Punctuation details

The following list gives examples of the most commonly used types of referencing using this referencing style.

1 Single author
   Vane, H. (2019). *The cost of chaos: The dark side of organisational planning.* University of Michigan Press.
2 Single author, later edition
   Campion, A. (2017). *Embracing uncertainty: Report writing as a creative art* (3rd ed.). Prentice-Hall, Inc.
3 Two authors
   Strunk, W., Jr., & White, E. B. (1999). *The elements of style* (4th ed.). Macmillan.
4 Corporate author
   American Psychological Association (2020). *Publication Manual of the American Psychological Association* (7th ed.). American Psychological Association.
5 Edited book
   O'Connor, R., & O'Connor, E. A. (Eds.). (2010). *Managing change in religious organisations.* Oxford University Press.
6 Article or chapter in edited book
   Mellallieu, P. J. (2011). The postmodernist manager. In P. J. Mellallieu & N. Boneparte (Eds.), *The manager: Missionary, magician and megalomaniac* (pp. 134–159). John Wiley and Sons.

How do I reference a periodical?

Periodicals are anything that is published on a regular basis: magazines, journals and newspapers. Sometimes it is difficult to distinguish between journals and magazines, but here is a general rule of thumb: if the articles in the periodical have a reference section (i.e. if they list their sources in some academically conventional way), then it can be regarded as a journal; if they do not have a reference section, then treat it as a magazine.

Periodicals are referenced as follows.

Titles of periodicals should be quoted in full and italicised (or underlined) and followed by volume numbers, italicised, and page numbers, not italicised. Titles of articles should not be italicised, underlined or placed in inverted commas. Include the DOI if one has been assigned to the journal article. If there is no DOI, add the URL.

1   Journal article, one author
    Frolov, D. (2021). Blockchain and institutional complexity: An extended institutional approach. *Journal of Institutional Economics*, *17*(1), 21–36. DOI: https://doi.org/10.1017/S1744137420000272

2   Journal article, multiple authors
    Baker, H. K., Kumar, S., & Pandey, N. (2021). Thirty years of Small Business Economics: A bibliometric overview. *Small Business Economics*, *56*(1), 487–517. https://doi.org/10.1007/s11187-020-00342-y

3   Magazine article
    Emerson, A. M. (2017, December). Bald is beautiful. *North and South*, 16.

4   Newspaper article, no author
    Locals attack Pike report. (2018, June 16). *The Dominion*, 3.

5   Newspaper article, author known
    Robinson, L. (2009, July 19). The new orthodoxy. *The Dominion*, 9.

How do I reference internet sources?

1   Article in an online newspaper
    Smialek, J. (2021, March 17). The financial crisis the world forgot. *Sydney Morning Herald*. https://www.smh.com.au/business/the-economy/the-financial-crisis-the-world-forgot-20210317-p57bd3.html

2   Web page
    Gale, A. (2021, March 11). *How to keep grounded as a leader*. Management Today. https://www.managementtoday.co.uk/keep-grounded-leader/leadership-lessons/article/1709743

A note regarding the author: if the web page does not have a specified author, see if you can find a corporate author. If neither is available, move the title into the author's position.

A note regarding date: if no date is available, place n.d. in the date position.

How do I reference research reports?

Technical reports usually include a report number which should be included in the reference, as shown in the following example.

Ministry of Business, Innovation & Employment (2021). *Canned Peaches from Greece Full Review: Stage 1 Final Report* (MBIE/AD/R/2020/003 Public File #038). https://www.mbie.govt.nz/dmsdocument/12977-canned-peaches-from-greece-2020-full-review-stage-1-final-report

How do I reference unpublished theses?

Frawley, E. A. (2017). *Nobody does it better; English administrators face their limitations* [Unpublished master's thesis]. Waikato University.

Knowles, G. A. (2018). *New methods for old* [Unpublished doctoral dissertation], Monash University.

How do I reference study guide or lecture material?

If you cite articles or excerpts from books that are provided on course websites, refer to the article or e-book directly (your study material *should* contain full bibliographical information!).

If the material being cited is not part of an article or e-book, it should be referenced as follows.

Fordyce, S. (2011). *Ethics and canon law* [PowerPoint slides]. http://www.legalethics/pages/law/ppt/fordyce-prof.ppt

Note that most teachers prefer that you go to outside academic sources rather than just relying on study guide material, to demonstrate that you can explore the topic outside the boundaries of the course material. If you do need to reference the study guide or lecture notes, it is important that you also include other sources in your assignment, unless your tutor or lecturer has specifically said that this is not necessary.

How do I cite an Act of Parliament?

APA is a North American system, and so it provides no official set of conventions for referencing New Zealand or Australian legislation. Based on the principles of APA conventions, the following approach is suggested:

Resource Management Act, No. 69. (1991). http://www.legislation.govt.nz/act/public/1991/0069/latest/whole.html

How do I cite a video?

1   YouTube video

Crash Course (2016, November 22). *Utilitarianism: Crash Course Philosophy #36* [Video]. YouTube. https://www.youtube.com/watch?v=-a739VjqdSI&list=RDQMsy-gkNaAsqk&start_radio=1.

2   TED talk

   Awuah, P. (2007, June). *How to educate leaders? Liberal arts*. TED Conferences.
   https://www.ted.com/talks/patrick_awuah_how_to_educate_leaders_liberal_arts

How do I cite a personal communication?

Sometimes you will need to acknowledge personal communication as a source of information. This includes lecture notes, memos, email messages, interviews and the like. Personal communication is *not* included in a reference list or bibliography – you should only cite personal communications in the text of your assignment.

Where do I find information about referencing materials not mentioned here?

For details on how to format other, more unusual material (e.g. proceedings of meetings and symposia, films, TV programs, individual interviews), refer to the *Publication Manual of the American Psychological Association* (7th ed.), also referred to as the APA Style Manual. The APA website provides details and examples: https://apastyle.apa.org/style-grammar-guidelines/references/examples

What is a bibliography?

As mentioned above, a reference list should contain *only* the material you have cited in your text. If other material as background reading has been used it may be included in a new list called the bibliography. Format the material in exactly the same way as in the reference section. Note: it is not necessary to include a bibliography in an assignment – most assignments will only use a reference list. Provide a bibliography only where there are other sources that have influenced your thinking, but you have not cited or quoted from them.

Check your understanding

1. What is plagiarism? Can you find your institution's policy on plagiarism or academic misconduct/integrity? What are the penalties for plagiarism? Write out the definition of plagiarism used by your institution and place it in a prominent position on the wall near your desk.
2. Why does referencing matter?
3. What system of referencing is used by your college or department? If it doesn't use APA, bookmark on your computer one of the appropriate websites listed in this chapter.
4. Why do you need to be precise about referencing conventions?
5. If you are using a single authored journal article for an assignment, what bibliographical data do you need to record for referencing purposes?

6. Does your institution provide a referencing tool such as EndNote to students at a discount rate? Does the library or learning centre run tutorials on using EndNote? Why are referencing tools useful?
7. Find an unusual source (a radio interview, a data set, an Instagram page, for example) and check on the APA referencing website to see how to reference it.

Helpful resources

A brilliant tool and website that will help you understand how to use secondary sources in your writing: https://www.cite.auckland.ac.nz/index.html

A comprehensive website that will enable you to understand a range of approaches to referencing: https://owl.purdue.edu/owl/research_and_citation/resources.html

APA main page on using in-text citations. This provides more detail and tips for referencing using APA conventions: https://apastyle.apa.org/style-grammar-guidelines/citations

A Using secondary material

One of the main differences between school-based assignments and academic assignments is the requirement that you place your argument or analysis within a scholarly context – that is, you cite the ideas of other authors. Incorporating the ideas of other writers into your own work is a skill you need to learn if you are to achieve satisfactory grades.

Terminology

First of all, let us look at some terms that relate to using sources in assignments.

Academic or secondary source

An academic source (or a secondary source) refers to any piece of material used when writing an assignment on a particular topic. This may include a journal article, a newspaper article, a book, a blog, a website or a news interview – anything that influences your discussion of a particular topic.

Quoting

A quotation is an exact copy of a passage from another source – it is a word-for-word transcript of someone else's words. If a quotation is used, you must indicate in the text that this is a quotation (by indenting the passage or placing it in inverted commas) and it must be referenced correctly (for more detail about this, see Chapter 13).

Citing or paraphrasing

Citing involves using someone else's ideas or data but expressing those ideas in your own words. For example, imagine you are writing an assignment for a business communications course on how we interpret others' comments. You come across this line from a book by Rosenwasser and Stephen (2018):

> An interpretation is a theory, a hypothetical (still open to question and testing) explanation of what something means.

As part of your assignment, you decide it is important to have a definition of the word 'interpretation'. You like the ideas expressed by Rosenwasser and Stephen, but, in order to write fluently, you choose to use your own words rather than quoting them – that is, you choose to cite or paraphrase their words. Here is one way it might be done:

It is important, for the purposes of this essay, to have an understanding of what 'interpret' means. According to Rosenwasser and Stephen (2018), an interpretation is not a fixed position. Instead, it is a tentative, hypothetical idea, which is still being tested, about what someone has said or written.

Note that when citing information, the source still needs to be acknowledged. Again, refer to Chapter 13 for more detail on how to reference citations.

Plagiarism

Plagiarism is a very serious matter, and it is vital that you understand what it means. We may define plagiarism as:

> Presenting as one's own work the work of another, including copying or paraphrasing of another's work without acknowledging it as another person's work through full and accurate referencing; it applies to material presented through written, spoken, electronic, broadcasting, visual, performance or other medium.

Note that plagiarism in assignments involves any of the following:

- Inserting whole text from another source (e.g. journal or website) and not acknowledging the source.
- Inserting whole text from another source (i.e. quoting it) and providing a reference, but not indicating that it is a full quotation.
- Inserting whole text from another source but changing occasional words. Even if you acknowledge the source, you have still plagiarised. If you want to cite another source, you must change it *entirely* into your own words.
- Copying an assignment or part of the assignment from someone else (classmate, someone who took the course in a previous semester). Even if you change the words but the sentences still convey exactly the same ideas in the same order, this is plagiarism.
- Two people working together and submitting the same, or a very similar, assignment as individual work.
- Not acknowledging a citation. Remember, if you put someone else's ideas into your own words, you must still acknowledge the source.
- Resubmitting an assignment (or part of an assignment) that you've already submitted for another course. This is called *self-plagiarism*.
- Submitting an assignment written by someone else as your own.

Any form of plagiarism is considered to be 'academic misconduct' and is viewed seriously by all tertiary institutions. You must take all warnings about plagiarism seriously; in some cases the consequences can involve failing your course or having your misdemeanour recorded on your academic record.

While a few students do cheat intentionally, many more plagiarise by accident, because they don't understand how to reference correctly or because they are careless with other sources. Make sure you read this Appendix very carefully as well as Chapter 13.

Other students plagiarise because they run out of time, and the only way they can get an assignment in on time is by cutting and pasting from other sources. *You must never do this!* It is better to ask for an extension, or hand your assignment in a day late and pay a small penalty, than to jeopardise your whole academic career or academic record. Time management is the key here, but if you're caught short of time for some reason, talk to your tutor and see if an extension can be arranged.

Most institutions nowadays use plagiarism detection systems such as Turnitin. You have nothing to worry about with these systems as long as you are careful to use correct referencing conventions – indeed, it can be a helpful way of ensuring you are using sources correctly. We will return to Turnitin later in this chapter.

Why does plagiarism matter so much?

Plagiarism can be seen as a form of stealing or fraud – that is, you are passing off someone else's ideas as your own. In the academic world this really matters because new ideas or new findings are the currency of academic life. So, learning not to plagiarise (whether intentionally or not) is part of your learning to be part of an academic community.

But avoiding plagiarism also matters because you're here to learn. If you copy the ideas of other people or disguise the fact that someone else has written the assignment, then you're not learning anything about your course or about the topic. Your teachers want to hear your ideas, your thoughts and how you justify those ideas by drawing on, and acknowledging, the ideas and findings of other people. They want you to be able to form ideas and explain them – they want you to learn how to think critically and express yourself confidently.

When to reference citations

Referencing citations can cause problems for students: how do you decide what should be referenced? What if you are dealing with a very common and widely known issue? For example, you read in a book that 'communication is the lifeblood of the modern organisation' and you want to express this idea in your assignment. But surely it is such a widely held view that it does not warrant referencing? Should this idea be referenced?

If you are writing a report for a particular audience (e.g. the marketing manager of a company), you can answer this question simply: if the person you are writing for is likely to be generally familiar with the idea, then you probably do not need to reference it.

However, an essay is more difficult to assess because your audience is not so clearly defined. Perhaps an analogy would help.

Imagine you are playing for a club cricket or netball team, and you are discussing strategies for an upcoming game with team mates. Everyone in the group will know certain things: what the rules of the game are, what the names of the positions are, whether you are playing home or away. In the same way, when you are writing an essay in a particular discipline, certain pieces of knowledge are shared information. These do not need to be documented for the same reason that you do not take the time to explain to your team mates what a wicketkeeper or goal keeper is.

However, in your meeting, some things will be known only to one person. The captain may have played the opposing team before and remembers a weak player; another player may remember that the pitch tends to be slow, even in midsummer. These ideas are expressed by single voices; they are not shared knowledge and so should be attributed to particular sources.

Documenting an essay works in the same way. For example, it is common knowledge among people working in business communication that men and women use language differently. But some researchers have identified *how* men and women use language differently. If you find an author who does discuss specific differences or presents data showing, for example, that men interrupt more, then you would reference that source.

Once you become familiar with a subject area, you will develop a sense of what needs to be referenced. But, if in any doubt, provide a reference; you are unlikely to be penalised for providing too many.

How to use sources

The next skill to develop is a judgement of *how* to use other authors in your work. Reports and essays use secondary sources quite differently.

Essays

A problem commonly raised by students is: 'How much does my lecturer want to know what *I* think, or do they just want to hear what everyone else has said?' It is an interesting question – and not easily answered (try asking one of your lecturers some time).

Your lecturer, generally, *does* want to know what you think. But they want to know what you think *in the context of the scholarly debate on the topic*. To use a musical analogy, they want to hear you play the solo instrument, but with the whole jazz band supporting you in the background.

An important point to realise is that there is an academic debate on every scholarly subject. Your marker wants you to position yourself within that debate. So, your essay should define the parameters, the points in between *and where you stand in the debate* (and why).

Take, for example, an essay on the following topic:

Define the usefulness of the concept of the product life cycle.

As you read other writers on the topic, you find some who think the product life cycle is the most valuable tool in a marketer's armoury. You will find others who say it is, and always has been, a totally useless concept. And you will find still others who say it is useful to a certain extent but has some limitations. Weighing up the evidence, you think it *is* useful (for purposes X and Y) but of little use as a predictor.

The whole thrust of your essay, then, should be to explain and defend *your* position. But you should also explain who is on the perimeters of the debate and what the other positions are. If you have allied yourself with another writer, explain why you find their evidence so compelling and the others' evidence limited.

To go back to our earlier jazz band analogy, your thesis statement (and the defence of that thesis statement) is your solo; the jazz band is composed of the ideas of others, and all these parts, solo and background instruments, are vital to the work as a whole.

Place yourself somewhere in the debate

Reports

Because the purpose of a report is invariably *practical* (i.e. what should be done in a certain situation), you use the ideas of other authors to support your own practical observations.

Practical observation	The organisation has grown so rapidly in response to customer demand that the company's strategic plan (which was always vague and non-specific) is now almost totally irrelevant and inapplicable. Thus the company
Backup from another source	lacks direction; as Anderson et al. (2009) observe, a bad plan will cause the organisation to suffer.

Academic sources are used in the discussion section of your report to back up your practical analysis and solutions. They show the reader that you have some credibility, authority and weight behind your statements. In the above example, you are showing that you are not alone in thinking that poor planning can cause problems – other authorities have noted poor planning as a problem for other organisations.

Note that for academic reports to a client, you will be expected to use in-text references in your Discussion section and possibly, but not necessarily, in the Introduction (e.g. where you introduce the context). It would be very unusual to include in-text references in the Conclusions and Recommendations section as well.

For research reports, the primary place for your in-text references is in the Literature review and Discussion. You may also find it appropriate to include them (but again, not necessarily) in the Introduction and Conclusion.

Turnitin

Many tertiary institutions now have a licence to use Turnitin (see http://www.turnitin.com). Turnitin is a commercial website that can scan an assignment, or any document, to identify how the document has incorporated other sources into its text. It is a powerful tool for identifying plagiarism, but can also be used to examine how a writer has used sources. Turnitin produces a colour-coded *similarity report* for each submitted document which shows where a writer has used secondary sources.

Many classes put all student assignments through Turnitin. In this situation, Turnitin can also check whether a student has used identical wording to someone else in the class, or whether a student has used the same wording as someone in another class (e.g. someone who took the class a year ago).

Different instructors use Turnitin differently. Some instructors use Turnitin as a way of *policing plagiarism*: students are required to submit their assignments to Turnitin when they submit the assignment online. The instructors then check the Turnitin reports themselves and use Turnitin to identify plagiarism and provide evidence on which to base penalties.

Other instructors will use Turnitin in a more *educational manner*: they look at the similarity reports to check whether their students understand how to integrate other sources into their text and they use the similarity reports to show students how to use sources more effectively.

Other instructors use Turnitin as an *enabling tool*: they allow students to submit to Turnitin and check the similarity reports themselves before they submit an assignment, so the students can check that they've avoided plagiarism.

Whatever way your teacher uses Turnitin, you have nothing to fear if you've understood and followed the ideas and instructions discussed in this Appendix and in Chapter 13. The key to avoiding plagiarism is to understand how to integrate sources into your text appropriately. If, after you've read this Appendix and Chapter 13, you still don't fully understand how to use sources in your writing, visit a student support or writing advisor on your campus, or read some of the online sources listed at the end of the Appendix.

Integration

Finally, a word about incorporating the ideas of others into your work.

Remember that any assignment you write should be an integrated whole. Quotations and citations should be worked into your assignment so that they become an integral part of it.

Never leave a quotation to stand alone or speak for itself. Introduce a quotation by letting the reader know your opinion of it: do you agree or disagree? Or do you feel that the author is only partially correct? Why? What are the limitations of this idea? How does this idea compare with someone else's? After the quotation, comment further or develop the idea in some way.

As a general rule, it is better not to use a quotation or citation in the first sentence of a paragraph. Instead, write the first sentence of the paragraph (which conveys the main idea of the paragraph) in your own words, and then back up that idea with quotations or citations.

As your experience in writing academic assignments grows, and as your knowledge of the subject you are studying develops, you will find that incorporating the ideas of others fluently and elegantly into your own work becomes easier. Like all aspects of writing, this is a skill that develops with practice.

Check your understanding

1. Locate your institution's plagiarism policy. If you are studying in a large institution, you should be able to find it on the institution's website. Alternatively, ask one of your lecturers or tutors if they have a copy you can see. Look at how the institution defines plagiarism. There are also likely to be different kinds of penalties for different kinds of plagiarism. Make sure you understand the principles behind the policy. Note: most institutions will not talk about a 'plagiarism policy' but rather an 'academic integrity' policy.
2. What is self-plagiarism?
3. Why does plagiarism matter?
4. Thinking about the subjects you are studying, what do you think would constitute 'common knowledge' in that subject?
5. Find out whether your institution has a licence for Turnitin and how the teachers in your institution use Turnitin.
6. Why do you think using sources is so important in tertiary study?

Helpful resources

There are some useful resources that will enable you to scan for plagiarism in your own work. Examples are Grammarly: https://www.grammarly.com/plagiarism-checker and Quetext: https://www.quetext.com

Turnitin provides some useful articles about plagiarism: https://www.turnitin.com/solutions/plagiarism-prevention

This webinar is especially useful in explaining how to read a Turnitin report: https://www.turnitin.com/events/virtual/how-to-interpret-a-turnitin-similarity-report-2

Purdue OWL has a great flow diagram on how to decide whether you should cite something or not: https://owl.purdue.edu/owl/avoiding_plagiarism/should_i_cite_this_poster.html

The Massey OWLL has many tips, including how to avoid plagiarism anxiety: https://owll.massey.ac.nz/referencing/plagiarism.php

A useful video is found here: https://www.jcu.edu.au/students/learning-centre/academic-integrity/what-does-plagiarism-look-like

B Paragraphing, punctuation and pretentiousness – elements of style

What is said and how it is said can be equally important in creating a successful assignment. This section focuses on three key elements of academic writing: paragraphing, punctuation and appropriate academic style.

Paragraphing

Paragraphing technique can be the factor that transforms a page of muddled ideas into a page of reasoned, logical prose. It is wise to stick to a simple paragraphing style when writing at an undergraduate level, where clarity of thinking and presentation are vitally important. The following principles should guide the way paragraphs are written for undergraduate assignments.

Every paragraph should contain a single developed idea

Paragraphs are the building blocks of an assignment. If each paragraph develops one idea fully, the reader will have the opportunity to read and consider one idea at a time. If there is more than one idea in a paragraph, the reader is likely to be confused – or may miss one of the ideas.

The key idea should be stated in the opening sentence

This is called using a *deductive* paragraphing style. Because the reader's attention tends to be most focused at the beginning of a chunk of writing, it seems sensible to state a key idea at the beginning of a paragraph. This key idea is called a *topic sentence*. This paragraph and the one preceding it are written in a deductive style.

The rest of the sentences can then develop, explain and support the topic sentence. It is a good idea to write the topic sentence in your own words rather than using a quotation.

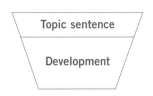

Use a variety of methods to develop your topic sentences

There are many ways to develop an idea. Here are a few of them. Note that each paragraph example is written in a deductive style (i.e. the topic sentence comes *first*).

Develop your topic sentences using:

* *Descriptive or factual details.* This method of paragraph development involves giving a more thorough, concrete explanation of the idea expressed in a general way in the topic sentence. Factual details give measurable, observable or historical information

that can be verified. Descriptive details give specific characteristics of the subject being discussed. For example:

> Planning is a vital aspect of every organisation. It gives a company direction and a sense of purpose. It draws all members of the organisation together and makes every decision clearer. Without planning, an organisation may founder either through lack of direction or through divisive directions.

- *Illustrations and examples.* The writer may use several brief examples or one extended illustration. The illustration may be factual or hypothetical (i.e. invented for the purpose of illustration). For example:

> Planning is a vital aspect of every organisation. For Southern Motors, a designer of small engines in New Zealand, it was a life-saver. The company was foundering for lack of direction, trying to fill needs in conflicting markets. When the new general manager, Colin Appleyard, was appointed, his first step was to draw all the operational managers together to construct strategic and tactical plans. The decision was made to halve the number of products and to target specific markets. Now, three years later, the company is going from strength to strength.

- *Definitions.* These can be used to explain concepts or terms that may be unfamiliar to the reader. It is generally more effective to attempt your own definition rather than copying from a dictionary. A definition is often more effective when combined with an illustration or example. For example:

> Planning is vital to all organisations. Planning is a broad term. It involves many processes – forming a mission statement, designing a strategic plan, defining goals and establishing operational methods. It has implications for every level of the organisation.

- *Authority.* It is common to use authority to develop the topic sentence. This is appropriate and useful because it positions your work within an academic debate – it shows that your idea is supported by people who may have more credibility and standing than you do. For example:

> Planning is vital to all organisations. Sanders (2003) sees it as 'the skeleton of the organisation, determining the structure and capabilities of a company' (p. 16). Other researchers (Carlton, 2004; Fiach & Paine, 2008) emphasise its capacity to create a sense of direction and unity.

Make sure you develop your paragraphs fully. Very short paragraphs should only be used when you want to make an impact statement (i.e. where you want to make an idea really stand out for the reader). If you find yourself writing lots of short paragraphs, check to see whether you are supporting and developing your topic sentences sufficiently.

Use connectives between and within paragraphs to unify your writing

Words that signal logical relationships between ideas also help to clarify the message for the reader. In analytical writing, each sentence and paragraph should be related logically to the sentence or paragraph that precedes or follows it. This connection is often implicit in the writing. Good writers also have an extensive vocabulary of connectives that signal explicitly the relationships between sentences and paragraphs. These connectives clarify your line of thought for the reader. Six types of logical relationships are set out in Figure 1.

Logical connective	Examples
Signals for addition	another point is, in addition, likewise, moreover, similarly, furthermore
Signals for change of direction	despite this, instead, nonetheless, nevertheless, on the other hand, however, alternatively
Signals signifying a logical relationship	therefore, as a result, accordingly, because of this, hence, consequently, thus
Signals for specific illustration or example	for example, for instance, to illustrate
Signals of a number of points	firstly, secondly ..., a further point is

Figure 1 In-text highlighting in combination with a bulleted list

If concise, clear writing is required, using a short connective (i.e. a word or short phrase) at the beginning of the topic sentence of a paragraph is probably the best way to show the logical connection between two paragraphs.

But if *flow* or *fluency* are important in your writing, then you might instead choose to use connective sentences *at the end* of your paragraphs, like this:

Intuition is a key theme running through the literature on expert behaviours.	topic sentence
Dreyfus and Dreyfus (1988), Benner (2004), and Dall'alba and Sandberg (2006) all highlight the importance of intuition in the decision making of experts. Indeed, for Dreyfus and Dreyfus (1988, 2004), it is the critical factor that distinguishes the responses and praxis of experts from those of competent or proficient professionals. And this ability to respond intuitively clearly distinguishes the fluid response of the expert in comparison to the lock-step, rule-following	development
behaviour novice. Generally, then, researchers are in agreement about the importance of the intuitive behaviour of experts.	summary
There is, however, another perspective and this is provided by Bereiter and Scardamalia (1987, 1993).	connective
Bereiter and Scardamalia, in their ground breaking book on expertise, challenge the whole notion of intuition. Instead they suggest that	topic sentence
different forms of knowledge (e.g. hidden knowledge and self-regulatory knowledge) are at least as important as what they term 'impressionistic knowledge'.	development

Note that, in this example, the use of a connective sentence at the end of a paragraph means that the second paragraph flows very naturally from the first. This style of indicating the relationships between ideas leads to a much more fluent and, some might say, elegant form of writing than writing that is simply signposted by connective words or phrases at the beginning of each paragraph.

Punctuation

Students are sometimes tempted to think that punctuation is unimportant, the domain of fussy English teachers with nothing better to do than enforce meaningless rules. In fact, punctuation is important in keeping the meaning of a sentence clear. Consider, for example, the following sentences:

> The report which was written by Michael was shown to the Chairman of the Board.

> The report, which was written by Michael, was shown to the Chairman of the Board.

Writing should conjure up a picture in the reader's mind. Do you think the picture raised in the reader's mind by the two sentences above is the same or different? Hopefully you will see that they raise different images. In the first example, the suggestion is that there were several or many reports but only the one written by Michael was shown to the Chairman of the Board. In the second version of the sentence, there is only one report and that report is shown to the Chairman of the Board.

As a business student, you should understand the importance of clarity and precision, and punctuation is an important way to achieve this.

Punctuation is especially important if you write long sentences. Most of us learn to use punctuation intuitively (i.e. we may not know the rules of punctuation, but we have a 'feel' for how they should be placed). This can lead to some interesting errors! This section is designed to help you check on the rules that you may have missed at school.

If you are writing a large document such as a research report or thesis, you may find a book such as Lynne Truss' *Eats, shoots and leaves* very useful. It is also a surprisingly entertaining read!

Punctuation can be categorised under four different categories as:

* stoppers (full stop, question mark and exclamation)
* linkers (colons and semicolons)
* intruders (commas, dashes and brackets)
* apostrophes.

Here we look at each of these categories in turn.

Stoppers

The full stop

A full stop is used to mark the end of a sentence.

* The product life cycle is a useful business tool.
* Strategic planning can make the difference between success and failure in a small business.

The question mark

Question marks are only used for *direct questions*:
* Why do men and women communicate differently?
* What are the ethical issues around marketing to children?
  They are not used for *indirect questions*, such as:
* Local government often questions why the general public does not understand the reasons for rates increases.

The exclamation mark

Use exclamation marks very sparingly in professional writing. They should be used only in two situations. First, to give a command or instruction:
* Write this down!
* Start the planning process!
  Second, you use exclamation marks to express strong emotion:
* Rate rises are an outrage!
  As you may imagine, it is rare to either express strong emotion or to give commands in business writing. So, every time you consider using an exclamation mark, check whether what you're writing is really an instruction or expressing strong emotion. If it doesn't do either of these things, delete the exclamation mark.

Linkers

Semicolons and colons are classified as linkers because they link ideas together. Many people do not learn to use semicolons or colons at school, but they are essential pieces of punctuation.

The colon

A colon tells you something is coming up. It is used in two primary ways. The first is to lead into a list, example or piece of information, like this:
* Good interviews involve three key elements: planning, perceptive questioning and clear job descriptions.
* The key information you need is this: the meeting cannot be held in the evenings because our chairman is not available after 7 p.m.
  The second key way in which colons are used is when the second half of the sentence tells you something significant or specific about the first part:

- He had a good excuse for his actions: vital information had been withheld from him.
- There is only one solution to poor management: education.

The semicolon

The effective use of the semicolon has been described as the mark of a good writer. Use the semicolon in two ways. First, to separate out lengthy items in a list:

- Effective interviews require the following: a clear job description, which enables the interviewers to have clear criteria for selection; the development of open-ended questions to allow the interviewee to reveal their skills and abilities; and multiple interviewers, to enable the triangulation of perspectives.

The other important use of a semicolon is to join complete sentences which are linked by an idea. For example:

- He worked hard; the report was a great success.

By using a semicolon rather than a full stop here, you imply that these two ideas are linked together; in other words it is implied that the report was a success *because* he worked hard.

Note that you cannot use a comma to link complete sentences; always use a semicolon for this purpose.

Intruders

Commas, brackets and dashes are often used to add something to a basic sentence. For this reason, we call them intruders.

Commas

There are several reasons to use a comma. The main uses of a comma are outlined here.

Use a comma to add a word or phrase to the beginning of a basic sentence, such as:

- The dairy in ustry is critical to the overall wellbeing of our economy.

Add something to the beginning using a comma:

- Unfortunately, the dairy industry is critical to the overall wellbeing of our economy.
- Despite views to the contrary, the dairy industry is critical to the overall wellbeing of our economy.

Use commas to add something into the middle of a basic sentence. Here is that sentence again:

- The dairy industry is, despite views to the contrary, critical to the overall wellbeing of our economy.
- The dairy industry, while seen as overblown by some commentators, is critical to the overall wellbeing of our economy.

Use a comma to link two complete sentences that are joined by a conjunction (e.g. 'and' or 'but'):

- I did visit the factory, and I was invited to return later in the year.

Finally, use a comma to separate out short items in a list:

- Employers are looking for the following skills: literacy, team work and leadership potential.

Dashes

Dashes are often overused and should be used sparingly in professional documents. The primary use of dashes in professional writing is to indicate an important intrusion into a basic sentence:

* The dairy industry – which many consider over-regulated – is critical to the overall wellbeing of our economy.

You would use dashes to add an intrusion into this sentence if you wanted to emphasise the intrusion. If you didn't want to emphasise the intrusion, you would use commas instead.

The only other use of a dash in professional writing is to add an afterthought, like this:

* Most people without training in business communication write in very long sentences – and this is never a good idea.

Don't overuse dashes. They make your writing feel breathy and unsteady. Learn to use commas, semicolons and colons effectively instead.

Brackets

Brackets are used to add information that is considered subsidiary or not at all important to the sentence:

* All the rules of effective business communication (which we know are vital) are contained in this book.

Apostrophes

Apostrophes cause people a lot of confusion. At times it is claimed that the apostrophe is no longer useful and should be abolished. But that day has not yet arrived, and so, for the purposes of clarity and professionalism, you need to learn to use an apostrophe correctly.

Use an apostrophe when a letter (or more than one) has been left out of a word or phrase:

* She's (she has) mastered all the skills needed here.
* He won't (will not) attend lectures.
* It's (it is) going to work out well.
* It's (it has) been a worthwhile venture.
* You're (you are) going to meet the executive on Friday.

The main thing that trips people up is the second rule of apostrophe usage: you use an apostrophe to indicate *possession*. In other words, you use apostrophes to show that something belongs to something or someone else.

To indicate possession for *singular nouns*, add 's:

* There was an increase in the company's profits (the profits belonging to one company).
* The manager's attitude was unfortunate (the attitude belonging to one manager).
* Dr Gilbert's ideas are revolutionary.
* The zoo's management is exemplary (the management of one zoo).

To indicate possession for *plural nouns formed by adding s*, just add ':

* I noticed a change in all the trainees' responses (the responses of several trainees).
* The companies' profits were unchanged (the profits of more than one company).

Apostrophes are not yet extinct

To indicate possession for *plural nouns formed in other ways*, add 's:

- There was a real surge in the market for women's clothes.
- He has a selection of children's toys in his office.

    You do *not* need to use an apostrophe when referring to decades:

- This is a deeper recession than that of the late 1980s.

    You also do *not* need an apostrophe when making a plural of a word ending in a vowel:

- The market is the best place to buy locally grown tomatoes and potatoes.

    There are extra rules for using apostrophes in exceptional circumstances, but they are beyond the scope of this short overview. Refer to one of the resources at the end of this Appendix for more detail.

Style

Finally, this Appendix ends with a few words about the style of academic writing. Style is a difficult issue to define and explain. Remember that, even in academic writing, the main concern should be to communicate your ideas clearly to a reader. Style, then, should be designed on the basis of three things:

- the nature of your message
- the purpose of the sender
- the needs of the reader.

    Most academic writing at an undergraduate level (essays in particular) should be aimed at an audience that is intelligent but not well informed on your subject.

    In particular, these guidelines should be followed:

Speak to your audience

- Sentences should be short and they should contain a single idea.
- Write in the active voice.
- Cut out any unnecessary words.
- Do not use personal pronouns (I, we, you) unless you are told you can.
- If there is a choice between a long word and a short word, choose the short word.
- If jargon is used, define the terms.
- Use gender neutral and culturally safe language.
- Be direct.
- Aim for clarity.

The last point is perhaps the most important, and incorporates many of the other items on the list. Do not make the mistake of thinking that complex sentences, a pretentious, convoluted style and long words will impress the reader. Such a style is more likely to obscure your ideas. Write in a simple, clear, yet formal manner, using language that you fully understand, and you will communicate with the reader.

Check your understanding

1. Why do you think it is important to write in deductive paragraphs?
2. Find a piece of writing and delete all the connective words and phrases. What is the effect of this on the writing?
3. Do you think that your main aim in writing for your discipline is conciseness and clarity or fluency and flow?
4. How were you taught punctuation skills at school? Are there any errors you know you often make? If so, look at some of the following resources and see if you can improve your skills.
5. What do you think it means to say you should write in a gender neutral and culturally safe way?

Helpful resources

General reading on punctuation

Truss, L. (2003). *Eats, shoots and leaves: The zero tolerance approach to punctuation.* Profile Books.

Venolia, J. (2001). *Write right* (4th ed.). Ten Speed Press.

11 ways to tune up grammar and punctuation: https://www.dummies.com/careers/find-a-job/11-ways-to-tune-up-grammar-and-punctuation

Apostrophes

The Purdue OWL has a great section, with exercises, on punctuation. Here is the link to the exercises on apostrophes: https://owl.purdue.edu/owl_exercises/punctuation_exercises/apostrophes/apostrophes_exercise.html

Reading on academic style

There are some great free online tools to improve your writing. Grammerly (https://www.grammarly.com) can be very helpful, or try The Writer's Diet (https://writersdiet.com).

Monash University provides some useful exercises in academic style: https://www.monash.edu/rlo/research-writing-assignments/writing/features-of-academic-writing/academic-language

A style manual can be helpful – e.g. Hacker, D., & Sommers, N. (2021). *A pocket style manual* (9th ed.). Bedford/St Martin's.

A useful video on academic style can be found here: https://www.youtube.com/watch?v=yi5tld98ePE

C Presenting data

Introduction

Using graphics in your reports is an excellent way of focusing your audience's attention on the points you are making and presenting your points in a manner that is easy for your audience to understand. But as graphics are also a great way to confuse or inadvertently mislead your audience, it is important that you know which type of graphic is appropriate to use, when to use it and how to use it. The rules and points of style that we will introduce you to in this appendix are fairly general, and are designed to get you started and confident in what you are doing. If your department, faculty or institute requires you to follow a specific style, then refer to the appropriate style manual.

There are two types of graphics: tables and figures. Tables are best suited to displaying specific, related facts, data or statistics in a small space. You can present data more concisely in tables than you can in text, and more accurately than you can achieve with figures. Detailed comparisons among different groups within the data are often easier to display in a table than in a figure, and nearly always easier to express than with text. On the other hand, figures are an excellent method of displaying trends, general comparisons, movements, distributions and cycles in your data.

Before introducing you to some of the finer points of tables and figures, let's pause to affirm the overarching principle of their use. Simply stated:

> Graphics should document or clarify, but not duplicate, data given in text or other graphics.

This means that you should never present a graph and a table of the same set of data, or give a verbatim description in your text of data that you have also presented in a graphic. Understand, however, that your text and graphics should interact with each other. A characteristic of good writers is their ability to link the graphics with the text, using their text to highlight, interpret and discuss the information in the graphics. If you remember nothing else in this appendix, remember this point.

Using tables

Informal tables

Books on writing style usually distinguish between two types of tables – *informal* and *formal*. An informal table is a euphemism for a simple list. To draw your audience's attention to an informal table, you can separate it from the text either by adding an empty line above and below the table, or by increasing margin space on both sides of the table, or both. Unlike formal tables (as you will soon see), informal tables do not have headings (titles), nor are they numbered. Usually, each line of the informal table will be bulleted. For example, if we were to summarise the main characteristics of informal tables in an informal table, we would note that informal tables are:

- separated from the main text by white space
- displayed without any headers or number
- bulleted (although this is an optional extra)
- just simple lists.

Formal tables

At first, you may not like constructing formal tables because they require more effort to build than simple informal tables. But do persevere in developing this skill because the value of formal tables for presenting complex information concisely, accurately and clearly more than compensates for the extra effort required in their construction. But before you expend the effort, make sure you decide whether or not a formal table is appropriate.

Use the following checklist to decide when a formal table is appropriate:

- You have more than six items of data to present. You can usually express in your text the relationships and meaning inherent in small numbers of data (i.e. fewer than six items) without having to resort to creating a table.
- There are more than two outcomes in your data. For example, if some categories of small businesses were still trading successfully after five years, while other groups had ceased trading, such information is better presented in your text.
- Your data actually contain important information. It is pointless, for example, to set up a table to present data that are not important to the report you are preparing. Tables are not the place to archive data (no matter how much time you took to collect them!).

The communicative value of a table depends on how well you link it with your text. It is *not* sufficient to just create a table without providing any reference to it in your text. Link your table to your text through an *interpretative translation* of the data in your table. In an interpretative translation, you discuss the highlights and interpret the main points of the table within a wider discussion of what the information in the table means to the topic of your report. Guide your readers through your table, but don't make the common mistake of literally repeating, in words, the content of the table. Vary the approach you make in linking your table to your text. It quickly becomes very tedious for your audience if they repeatedly meet such phrases as 'Table 1 shows that distributed practice resulted in fewer errors than did massed practice'. Instead, use alternative phrases to achieve the link; for example, 'Distributed practice resulted in fewer errors than massed practice (Table 1)'.

Building your table

There are two guiding principles of tables:

1 A table must stand independently of the text (i.e. you should be able to read a table and understand completely what it is about without having to refer to the text. The same rule applies to graphs and figures).

2 Organise the data so that the object(s) on which, or about which, the main data were collected reads down a single column, not across several columns.

Before explaining this by way of example, let's first refresh your memory of the basic anatomy of a formal table (Figure 1), and how these components are 'fleshed out' (Table 1).

The *number* of the table and its *title* always appear at the top of the table.	
The *boxhead* contains the column headings.	
The *stub* column(s) lists, row by row, the categories for which the information is being presented	The data being presented appear in columns in the *body* of the table.
Footnotes go in this section	

Figure 1 Five basic skeletal components of a formal table

In Table 1, the boxhead contains the headings for the categories in the stub column and the body of the table. The stub column contains the location variable. The body contains the data on the locations of internet access used by people in the different countries.

What are the other important features you should note about this table?

- The title is at the top of the table.
- The table is numbered.
- The use of lines is constrained – the lines that many word processors by default place around each cell in a table are distracting and usually quite unnecessary.
- Each row and column title starts with a capital letter.
- There is white space in the table – the data are not cramped together.
- The data in the columns in the body of the table are equally spaced.
- The data in the columns are decimally aligned.
- The unit of measure (in this case, %) is not repeated next to each data value in the body.
- A footnote presents a point of clarification of the source of the data.
- The table 'stands alone'; the reader does not need to refer to the text to understand the data.

Table 1 Comparison of places of access to the internet by country (% respondents)[a]

Location	Singapore	Indonesia	New Zealand	Australia	USA	Germany
Work	51	64	28	25	38	27
Home	63	21	59	57	71	48
School/ College/ University	12	15	15	19	22	15
House of friend or relative	3	14	14	9	21	2
Library	1	3	2	4	14	7
Other place	1	7	1	5	4	1

[a]adapted from Garton, 1999.

Now let's turn our attention to the importance of layout planning when constructing tables. Table 2 contains data on the percentage of finished goods to all manufacturing stocks (an indicator of whether the stocks have been entirely removed or merely pushed to another part of the manufacturing chain) in the automobile and combined manufacturing sectors in the United States of America and the United Kingdom over a period of years. In this table, the boxhead contains the headings for the categories in the stub column and the body. The stub column contains two variables (year and country) and the body contains the two manufacturing sector variables (all sectors combined, automobile). Notice that with this layout, it is very easy to compare the percentage of finished goods stocks between automobile and all manufacturing sectors for any combination of year and country.

Table 2 Comparison of finished goods stocks (%)[a] in the USA and UK manufacturing sectors, 1985–1992[b]

Year	Country	Manufacturing sector	
		All sectors combined	Automobile
1985	USA	32.5	13.2
	UK	29.7	58.0
1987	USA	31.7	17.1
	UK	30.4	57.1
1989	USA	31.6	19.5
	UK	32.0	62.9
1991	USA	32.9	16.2
	UK	33.0	60.6
1992	USA	34.3	15.7
	UK	32.6	59.6

[a]expressed as a percentage of all stock.
[b]adapted from Pilkington, 1998.

In Table 3, the same data used in Table 2 have been rearranged to make it easier to compare percentage of finished goods stocks between countries for each year and manufacturing sector combination.

Table 3 Comparison of finished goods stocks (%)[a] in the USA and UK manufacturing sectors, 1985–1992[b]

Year	Manufacturing sector	Country USA	UK
1985	All sectors combined	32.5	29.7
	Automobile	13.2	58.0
1987	All sectors combined	31.7	30.4
	Automobile	17.1	57.1
1989	All sectors combined	31.6	32.0
	Automobile	19.5	62.9
1991	All sectors combined	32.9	33.0
	Automobile	16.2	60.6
1992	All sectors combined	34.3	32.6
	Automobile	15.7	59.6

[a]expressed as a percentage of all stock.
[b]adapted from Pilkington, 1998.

Look at Table 4. This table contains the same data as Tables 2 and 3, but the layout is designed to aid comparison between countries for each year in each manufacturing sector.

Table 4 Comparison of finished goods stocks (%)[a] in the USA and UK manufacturing sectors, 1985–1992[b]

Year	All sectors combined USA	UK	Automobile sector USA	UK
1985	32.5	29.7	13.2	58.0
1987	31.7	30.4	17.1	57.1
1989	31.6	32.0	19.5	62.9
1991	32.9	33.0	16.2	60.6
1992	34.3	32.6	15.7	59.6

[a]expressed as a percentage of all stock.
[b]adapted from Pilkington, 1998

The important point to recognise in each of these examples is that it is easier to compare numbers in adjacent columns in the same row than numbers in adjacent rows in the same column. This means that you must carefully consider what are the important comparisons that you want to present to your audience.

So far, our discussion of tables has centred on the display of data. In business-orientated writing, tables are also commonly used as 'containers' for descriptive text (e.g. Table 5).

Table 5 Functions and information flows of distribution centres

Distribution centre operation	Description	Information flow
1 Receiving	Check, inspect and sign for all merchandise received	Bill of loading Package invoice
	Unload the merchandise	Purchase order
2 Movement to storage	Move merchandise to storage area	Movement ticket
3 Reserve storage	Put away	Storage location records
4 Order selection	Move to the designated area for order picking	Movement ticket Order picking ticket
	Order picking	Order selection location record updated
5 Repack	Pack the merchandise according to the order	Unit identification Packing invoice
6 Preparing for shipping	Check the shipping information	Packing invoice
	Mark any necessary container, box or pallet	Stock record updated
7 Loading	Load the merchandise to the vehicle	Bill of loading (or a manifest) List of shipments carried out by each vehicle

Notice how the same rules we set for tables containing data are also applied to text tables. For example, the table has a title and each column has a heading, and the stub column contains the category variable (distribution centre operation), row by row, for the information variables (description, information flow) being presented. Also notice that the contents of each cell in the sub columns are vertically aligned to the top of the cell.

Using figures

Although the term *figure* can refer to a photograph, flowchart, map or diagram, we will focus on the most common type of figure, the graph. Quite simply, graphs present numerical data in visual form. Graphs are excellent devices to show trends or important patterns in your data, or to compare the relative responses of different groups (e.g. brand of goods, manufacturing process) to some factor (e.g. time, capital investment, marketing strategy). Remember, however, that if the data themselves are important, then present them in a table; you should not expect your audience to read data off the axes of a graph. The three main types of graph you are most likely to use are *pie* graphs, *line* graphs and *bar* graphs.

Pie graphs

Whenever you need to compare percentages of a single whole, then a pie graph (or pie chart) is the graph to use (Figure 2). Provided that you do not have too many wedges (i.e. categories), pie graphs are easy to interpret and have a strong visual impact.

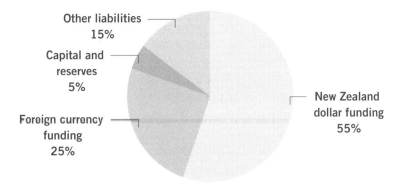

Figure 2 Distribution of balance sheet liabilities of registered banks in New Zealand, February 2009 (Data source: Reserve Bank of New Zealand)

The rules of style associated with these graphs are as simple as the graphs themselves:

- Make the relative percentages clear by starting at the 12 o'clock position and sequence the wedges clockwise.
- Sequence the wedges from largest to smallest (although sometimes this is not possible because it is difficult to clearly present the labels of small wedges adjacent to each other).
- Give the percentage value of each wedge, either inside each wedge or as part of the label.
- Keep all the labels horizontal.
- A simple font type (sans serif; e.g. Helvetica, Arial) is used.

Line graphs

You should use a line graph whenever you want to show the changes in the level or response of some variable (e.g. profit, stock numbers, value) against some form of continuous variable (e.g. time). Line graphs are particularly useful for comparing the relationship or trends between two or more groups of data (Figure 3).

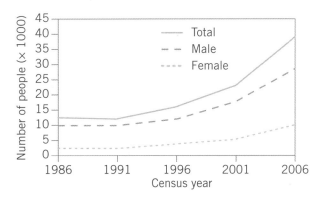

Figure 3 Numbers of population aged 65 years and over in full-time employment, 1986–2006 censuses (Data source: Statistics New Zealand, 2009)

There are several points to notice in this example of a line graph:

- The vertical (y) and horizontal (x) axes have simple, clear labels.
- The axis labels run parallel with the axes.
- A simple font type (sans serif; e.g. Helvetica, Arial) is used.
- The unit of measurement (i.e. mean number) of the variable plotted on the horizontal axis is clearly presented in the label.
- The three data sets (i.e. male, female and total unemployed) are distinguished from each other by the use of different lines (i.e. solid, dashed and dotted lines). You could also use different symbols to achieve the same purpose.
- A key for the distinguishing features is included in the graph.
- The title appears at the bottom of the graph.
- As well as the description of the graph, the title contains points of clarification of the data. (Compare this style to that of tables where such information is contained in the footnote section.)

Bar graphs

You'll find bar graphs very useful for presenting categorical data (i.e. data measured from separate groups of 'things' such as groups of people or income brackets, brands of goods, or type of treatment). Bar graphs share many style characteristics of line graphs: their vertical and horizontal axes are simply and clearly labelled; the units of measure are presented; and the title appears below the figure (Figure 4).

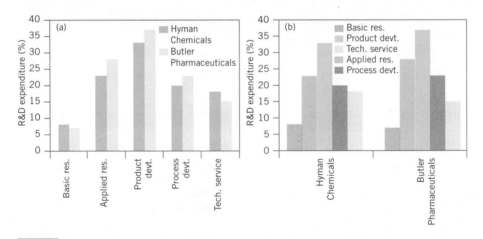

Figure 4 Comparison of allocation of R&D expenditure (%) between Hyman Chemicals and Butler Pharmaceuticals, 2004

Notice, in both Figures 4a and 4b, the space at each end of the horizontal axis to aid readability and, because both R&D category and company name are discrete variables (i.e. individually whole – you can't have 1½ companies), the gap between the bars of each level of these variables.

Figure 4 also demonstrates the importance of identifying the categories important to your comparison before you construct your bar graph. The same data set is used in both graphs, but whereas in Figure 4a the major category is 'R&D category' and the minor category is 'Company', these roles are reversed in Figure 4b. If your intention is to compare differences in R&D expenditure between companies for each R&D category, then Figure 4a is the correct layout. If, however, your focus is on within-company allocation of R&D expenditure, then Figure 4b is the best layout.

Bar graphs are usually presented with their bars in the vertical plane. However, placing them horizontally provides an easy-to-interpret means of presenting ordered data (i.e. categories ordered by magnitude of response or measure) (Figure 5). This ordered nature of horizontal bars is not an absolute requirement; it depends on the type of category or variable being plotted. For example, if the levels of the variable are discrete, then display the plot in order of magnitude of response. However, if the variable is continuous (e.g. time), then you must plot the data according to the magnitude of that variable.

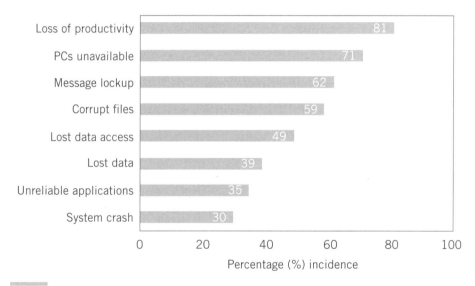

Figure 5 Relative effects of virus on computer function and operation (adapted from Hubbard and Forcht, 1998)

Notice the value at the end of each bar. This is a common practice with both horizontal and vertical bar charts when it is important to present data with precision and accuracy.

Horizontal bar graphs are also useful when displaying relative changes among categories as Figure 6 demonstrates. Notice how the categories ordered by magnitude (i.e. % change in land area planted; Figure 6a) allow the reader to more readily identify the categories with the largest increase (wine, grapes and avocados) and decrease (apples, other fruits and hops) in land area compared to the non-ordered categories (Figure 6b).

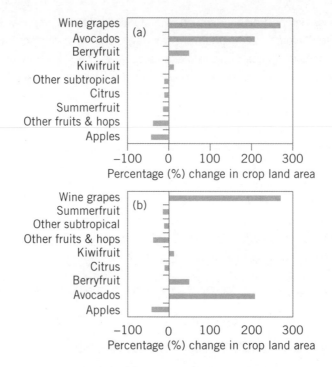

Figure 6 Percentage change (%) in land area planted with horticultural tree crops between 1996 and 2005/2006 in New Zealand (Data source: HortResearch, 2007)

One further variation of bar graphs is worth a quick mention. Stacked bar (or column) graphs (Figure 7) are particularly effective for comparing wholes (a weakness of the pie graph). In this example, regional managers exerted less influence over the approval of regional marketing budgets in 2008 than in 1998.

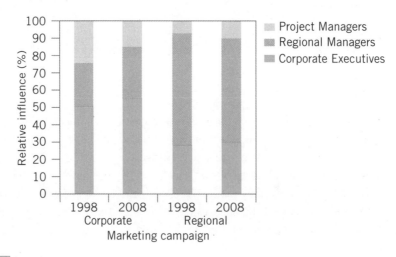

Figure 7 Relative influence of organisation hierarchy on approval of marketing budgets

Graphics abuse

Just as words can cloud meaning or mislead, so too can graphs. Try to avoid the following common errors when using graphics.

- Many graphics packages (particularly those associated with spreadsheet packages) offer you *line* and *X-Y* Scatter graphs. Line graphs differ from X-Y Scatter graphs in the way in which the levels of the variable on the horizontal axis are displayed. In line graphs, the levels are always equally spaced, regardless of their magnitude; in X-Y Scatter graphs, the spacing accurately reflects the magnitude of the level. Thus, if your horizontal axis is time (e.g. 1, 2, 5, 12 and 13 weeks), these will appear at equal spacing (incorrect) on a line graph and arithmetically spaced (correct) on an X-Y Scatter graph.

- Keep graphs as simple and uncluttered as possible. Many (spreadsheet) graphics packages, by default, produce grid lines at each major point on the vertical and horizontal axes. Such lines should be 'turned off' because they generally clutter up the graph, distracting your audience from its important information. Similarly, do not be seduced by the wide range of fancy variations of the basic types of graphs that are available in many graphics packages. For example, unless 3D bars actually improve the message of your bar graph, then do not use them (even if they are the default setting!).

- The default (and often the only) position for the title of the graph in many (spreadsheet) graphics packages is at the top of the graph. This position is not acceptable style for the reports you will write. Consequently, you will have to use your word processor to produce the title and description of your graphs in the correct position – below the graph!

- Many word processors allow you to print (wrap) text around one or both sides of your tables and figures. Just because the software allows this does not mean that this is an appropriate style. And for most, if not all, of the reports that you will prepare for your courses, wrapping text around tables and figures is not appropriate style.

- Make sure your figures are not ambiguous in the message they communicate. We all know that *a picture is worth a thousand words*, but don't forget that *a picture can hide a hundred 'truths'*. Look at Figure 8. Both plots use the same data set to plot the national consumption of beer and wine from 2001 through 2007. Which do you think is the best plot for showing relative changes in consumption patterns between beer and wine? The correct answer is neither! Figure 8a is not particularly informative; although it clearly shows the relative difference in overall consumption levels between beer and wine, it is difficult to accurately discern movements in beer and wine consumption individually. Figure 8b takes us to the other extreme. By placing the wine consumption data on the right-hand side vertical axis, and allowing both vertical axes to expand on different scales, we receive quite a different picture. Indeed, at first glance, it looks as though wine consumption has surpassed beer consumption! You have to look very closely at the actual consumption figures on each Y-axis scale to realise this is not what has happened – unfortunately, readers uneducated in interpreting graphs would jump to the wrong conclusion. So while Figure 8a hides the 'truth', Figure 8b distorts it. A better approach to comparing the relative changes in wine and beer consumption would be to calculate the percentage change in consumption in each year from 2001 and to display these data in a horizontal bar chart (Figure 6b) ordered by time.

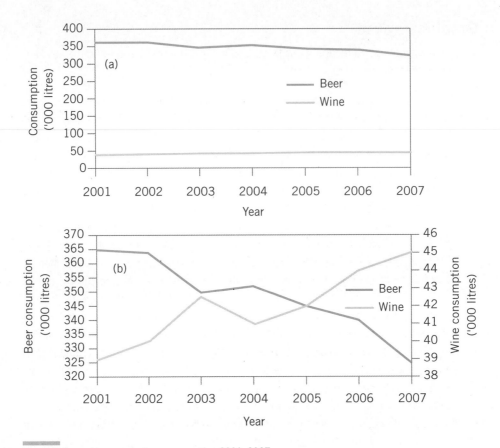

Figure 8 Annual beer and wine consumption 2001–2007

Figure 9 shows another method of distorting meaning. In this stacked area graph, profit is represented by the vertical distance from the top of the turnover area to the top of the profit area. In 1997, for example, profit was about $1.6 million. The dominant feature of this graph is the large, increasing area representing turnover. This upward trend makes the profit appear, at first glance, to be also increasing when in fact from 2003 onwards it is declining.

The message here is that you must remember that it is unfortunately easy using graphs to distort the true meaning of a data set. As a writer and a professional, you have an obligation to present information in a clear and unequivocal fashion. Always check your graphs for possible ambiguity before submitting your report or article. Better still, have a colleague peer-edit your writing – a fresh set of eyes will often find problems that your eyes won't.

Remember!

A final word about graphics (and yes, we have already mentioned this point, but it is important!). Remember that your audience deserves some guidance with your tables and figures. Do not follow the bad habit of many novice writers who lead their audience to a table or figure with a phrase such as 'The effect of organisation hierarchy on the approval of marketing budgets is shown in Figure 7', and then move onto the next point. Don't leave

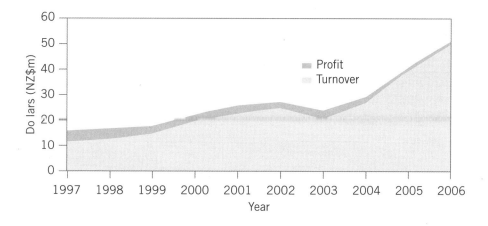

Figure 9 Turnover and profit trends over a 10-year period

your audience hanging on your graphics; guide them into the data. Tell your audience what you think the data have revealed (look at how we interpreted Figure 7). Remember that you are writing a report, not a crossword; your aim is to give a clear description, not to drop clues.

Check your understanding

1. What is the difference between a formal and an informal table?
2. What are the two guiding principles for designing a table? Why do these principles matter?
3. Look at Tables 2, 3 and 4. What are the differences between them? How would you choose which design to use?
4. When would you use a pie graph to present data?
5. How would you decide between using a line graph and a bar graph?
6. How might a figure or graph *disguise* information?
7. Is it easier to compare data on the same row in different columns or in different rows in the same column?

Helpful resources

Details on APA formatting for tables and graphs: https://owl.purdue.edu/owl/research_and_ citation/apa_style/apa_formatting_and_style_guide/apa_tables_and_figures.html

Useful summary of different styles of tables and graphs: http://www.mindtools.com/pages/ article/Charts_and_Diagrams.htm

Contains, among other tips and best practice approaches, a useful summary on how to select the most appropriate visual for your report: https://pressbooks.bccampus.ca/ technicalwriting/chapter/figurestables

D Exam skills

In the COVID and post-COVID era, universities and other institutions of higher education have had to completely rethink examinations. Many – if not most – have shifted to online examinations or to replacing traditional examinations with 'take-home' exams, which allow students to complete the examination offline over an extended period and then upload on the course website (or similar). Some programs may have done away with examinations altogether.

In this chapter, we look first at how to prepare for traditional examinations, then the newer forms of examination, and then additional issues such as dealing with stress.

The traditional exam

Two things are essential to exam success with traditional examinations (i.e. those sat under supervised conditions in a physical examination room):
- familiarity with the exam
- preparation of the material.

Familiarity with the exam

You may feel that, short of breaking into your tutor's office or computer, you cannot become familiar with the exam before you see it. Happily, this is not entirely the case: there are many things you can do to familiarise yourself with the exam before you walk into the exam room. Here are some useful strategies:

1 *If you are an internal student, studying on campus, always attend the last two weeks of classes.* Your tutor or lecturer is highly likely to advise the class on the exam, outlining what you should be studying, and possibly even the structure of the exam, in the last weeks of the course. Obviously, they are not going to tell you what the questions are beforehand, but they will provide you with lots of useful ideas: pay attention! Similarly, for all students, distance and internal, your teacher is likely to have given you hints on the exam in the study material: they may indicate where you should be focusing your preparation or include old exam papers. Teachers may also put resources on the class website or send out a class email about the exam: always take care to read this material carefully.

2 *Look at exams from past semesters.* Examiners generally use the same structure for all their exams (and if they're changing it this semester, they're likely to tell you in class), so this will give you valuable clues about the structure of the exam. Look at the *type* of questions asked: are they essays, short answers or multiple choice? Look at the *coverage* of the exam: are you going to have to know the whole course to pass the

exam or can you be selective? If the latter, then how much of the course do you have to know and how much choice do you have? Look at the *themes* that came up in past exams. Every topic within a course always contains key themes or main ideas, so look for these themes in the exam questions and how often they occur. You may be able to predict the kinds of themes (and therefore the kinds of questions) that are likely to occur in your exam.

3   *Think about timing.* Once you know the structure of the exam, work out your timing. If, for example, you have four essays to write in three hours, and each is worth the same number of marks (i.e. 25% each), you need to allow about 15 minutes for planning and checking, so you have about 40 minutes in which to write each answer. If you have a multiple choice section worth 50% of the marks and then two equally weighted essays, you've got 1½ hours to do the multiple choice section and 40 minutes for each essay. If you wait to work out your timing until you're in the exam, you waste valuable time; if you don't plan your time at all, you may spend most of your time on only part of the exam and thus lose valuable marks.

4   *Practise writing exam answers.* Once you've started working on the material for the exam, use some of the questions in old exam papers to test your knowledge. You might even like to practise writing the essays in the allotted time for the exam, so you gain confidence in writing under time pressure.

Preparation of material

Once you are familiar with what will be required in the exam, decide on a preparation strategy. Here are some ideas of how to do this.

1   *Scope out and then organise the material.* If you are going to have to be prepared to answer questions on all aspects of the course, then organise all your course material (lecture and tutorial notes, study notes provided by the lecturer, readings) into themes or subject areas. Read over all of it to get a feel for the course as a whole. If, on the other hand, you are only going to have to answer questions on, say, three topics in the course, prepare those sections you are going to answer questions on. *It is important that you prepare more than the bare minimum.* So, for example, if you are going to have to write on three topics, you should prepare four topics thoroughly and possibly a fifth in less detail. It is always possible that you will get a question that baffles you on your favourite topic, so you need some backup ideas on another topic.

2   *Read through each topic you'll need to know on the exam and write a summary document for each topic.* This summary document should be no more than one or two pages and should be strongly visual. Write out headings in bold and write lists of key supporting ideas. Or, if you are a strongly visual person, write your summary as a mind map. Design a page of notes so that, if you needed to, you could visualise it in the exam.

3   *Memorise as far as possible your summary document.* Use any technique that works for you: read it aloud, copy it out or write out essay topics that could relate to the topic.

4   *From time to time, go back to your notes for each topic and try to absorb more detail than is on your summary document.* You do need some detail, especially for multiple

choice questions, so don't neglect your more detailed material. Make sure you understand, and can write out, definitions or important models (if they're part of the course). Make sure you know what key authors have said on the topic.

The online exam

In this section, we talk about the online time-constrained examination. In many ways, this approach to examinations replicates the traditional exam, so all the advice about familiarisation and preparation described above applies to these kinds of examinations too. There are, however, some additional steps you need to take:

1 Do you need to download any new software for the examination? Some forms of online invigilated exams require you to download new software and have a webcam on your computer. Check this with your teacher or on the course website. Make sure you have downloaded the software and checked you have a webcam (some older computers may not have this built in, but if you can use Zoom or Skype video, then you're all good to go) *well before the exam date*. You do not want to be panicking at the last minute if there are technical glitches.

2 Check whether the exam is invigilated or not, and what kinds of materials (if any) or other forms of online access you're allowed into the examination. It is vitally important that you check this on the course website or by contacting your teacher – you do not want to inadvertently be accused of plagiarism because you didn't realise you weren't allowed resources in your exam.

3 It is possible that your teacher has had to devise an entirely new kind of exam with the move online, so past exam papers may not be so helpful to you. Make sure you read and attend to everything that your teacher says online or in (physical or online) classes about the structure of the exam.

4 Prepare your workspace. If you're doing an invigilated online exam and not allowed any resources, treat the exam workspace as you would any traditional exam – do not have your phone or any other kind of device with you. We are so used to accessing our phones regularly that it may be too much temptation to have it nearby. Do not have any study notes or resources on your desk. Completely clear your desk except for materials that you're allowed (e.g. a water bottle).

5 Prepare other people. Before the exam, prepare anyone in your household for the fact you cannot be interrupted. Put an 'Exam in Process' sign on your door.

6 In the unlikely event that something goes wrong during the exam that means you have a problem with completion (e.g. you lose internet connection), email or call your teacher right away. Explain the problem and ask what they can do to help. If something happens during the exam that may be mistakenly seen as cheating (e.g. someone comes into your room, despite all your preparation), email your teachers after the exam and explain how you handled the situation.

The 'take home' exam

This type of exam involves you being given the exam question(s), working on them at home and then submitting them within a specified period (e.g. 72 hours).

It's tempting to think that, because you have a longer period, you don't need to do the preparation required for a traditional exam. This would be a mistake. You still need to do all the preparation steps (apart from memorising) that are listed above for the traditional exam. At the very least, ensure you have organised (and, ideally, summarised) your notes and key ideas so that you can access them quickly and easily. Use brightly coloured tags to help you find key quotes, ideas or themes. If you're allowed to write on the books, write short summaries, key points or mind maps in key places in the book. Don't cover the book with writing – you'll never find what you're looking for. Be tactical about what you write and where.

Three additional things are important:

1   Make sure you are super clear about the time and day you have to submit the exam. If the exam must be submitted online, it's entirely possible that the portal for submission will close at exactly the specified time. There may be no extensions, or very heavy penalties for late submissions. Do not treat this as if it were an assignment – it MUST be submitted on time.

2   Do your work on your own. Do not work in a group. Examinations are individual work, and working together both wastes valuable time and leads to potential plagiarism in a situation where people are stressed (online examinations are commonly put through Turnitin like an assignment).

3   Even if your teacher says they don't need you to provide references, do not copy and paste from another source, *including an earlier assignment you've written*. If you do quote, put the quote in quotation marks as you would for an assignment. See the comment above about Turnitin.

A take home exam may seem like an easier kind of exam than an invigilated time-constrained exam. But it can produce other forms of stress. Students worry about the exact amount of time they should be working on it during the specified period, or the expectations of standards, given that they have access to resources. Please don't try to work on this exam for unreasonable periods of time. Get plenty of sleep, eat well, get some exercise – and write to the best of your ability without worrying about expectations.

Dealing with stress

Everyone experiences some stress when preparing for or sitting exams. It is useful to remember that some stress is helpful, and that it can actually improve your performance. Too much stress can prevent you from preparing effectively or thinking clearly in the exam. If you find yourself experiencing difficult symptoms, such as long-lasting headaches, overwhelming sleepiness, irrational thoughts or panic attacks, then you need to learn strategies to deal with stress. Here are some ideas:

1 *Preparation*. Developing a sensible study timetable and sticking to it will help you to overcome stress. Organisational skills are important, so plan ahead and take the time to familiarise yourself with the exam and prepare effectively, as detailed earlier.

2 *Physical activity*. Regular exercise is an excellent way of dealing with stress. At the very least, try to get 20 minutes of exercise a day. Even two short 15-minute walks per day will make a difference.

3 *Rest and sleep*. You can't study all the time. If you try to, it will increase your stress levels. You must build time for rest and recreation into every single day (even the day before the exam!). Doing something unrelated to study will relax you and allow your body and mind to recuperate from the work they're doing. If possible, try to engage in recreational activities that involve other people: if you're very stressed, then watching TV, playing computer games, surfing the net or even reading may not enable you to unwind because your thoughts might continually return to your study. Interacting with other people allows you to let go of your study material for a while. And you need rest: if you're not sleeping for seven hours a day most days you are likely to become overly stressed.

4 *Talk*. Talking about your anxieties is helpful. Tell someone supportive and encouraging (a friend or family member) how you're feeling. Or, if you're seriously stressed, consider talking to a counsellor. Many large institutions have counsellors available on campus.

5 *Study groups*. This doesn't work for everyone or in every situation, but consider studying with a group of classmates at the preparation stage. You can often get through more work this way, you get to explore ideas you might not have thought of, and you also get a chance to talk and let off steam. However, it is important, if you're going to take this approach, to work with students with the same motivation and aspirations as you have.

6 *Finding the positives*. Exams are an opportunity to show what you can do. But all too often we turn that thought around and worry instead about how the exam will expose what we can't do or what we don't know. We don't advocate 'magical thinking': if you haven't been attending class and haven't spent much time on revision, then no amount of positive thinking will help you. But if you have put in the preparation, then try to turn worrying thoughts ('I can't have done enough work!') into positive ones ('I have studied in an organised way and I know what's expected of me: I can succeed'). Surround yourself with positive people who will encourage you to look at exams in a positive light and who will help you build your confidence and capability.

If at all possible, try to see stress as your ally in exam preparation. Stress can make your mind more alert and more responsive in an exam. If you feel overly stressed in an exam, put your pen down or stop typing, lean back, and breathe deeply and steadily. After several deep, steady breaths, pick up your pen or return to your screen and read the question you're focusing on (i.e. just one question – not the whole paper) carefully. Concentrate on one thing at a time.

The exam essay (for invigilated exams)

- *If you have a choice of questions, quickly decide which ones you will answer.* Don't waste time by musing over the options. Once you've made a decision, don't go back and reconsider.

- *Always do the easiest essay first* (if you're writing more than one) and try to do it in less than the time you've allocated to it. Never, ever, go over time on the easiest question! If you go over time on the easiest question, then you won't have time to think through the more challenging questions. Every exam marker has stories of students who have written a long, brilliant answer for one question and then barely had time – or have not had time – to finish the exam. Don't make this mistake!

- *Plan out your essay.* That way you give yourself a sense of direction, and if you don't finish the essay (e.g. if you run out of time) the marker can still give you some marks for what is in your plan.

- *Answer the question.* Many students simply write down everything they can think about the topic. This approach should be avoided. Your essay needs to start with a short, direct thesis statement that answers the question.

- *Write in deductive paragraphs.* A lot of students don't write in paragraphs at all, and this means that the examiner may miss some of the points students try to make. Remember, your marker is working quickly, so you need to make it easy for them to identify the key points of your argument. It's useful to think of paragraphs in exam essays as extended points: make a statement at the beginning of the paragraph and briefly back it up. Then start the next paragraph. It is a good idea to leave a line break between paragraphs so the paragraphing is clear.

- *The conclusion of an exam essay should be very brief* – a simple summing up is all that is needed. An eloquent and effective ending is not required in an exam.

- *In a traditional exam, at the end of your essay, leave ½–1 page clear*, so that if you suddenly remember another point, you've got space to include it.

- *When you've finished the essay do not read it through* – wipe the thoughts related to that essay out of your head and go straight onto planning the next one.

- But *remember that you have allowed some time at the end for checking.* This is when it is appropriate to read through and check each essay – quickly. Make sure your writing is legible and that you've included all your main ideas.

Check your understanding

1. List, in your own words, what you think are the most important things to do *before* a traditional exam.
2. How should your preparation for an online invigilated exam differ from that of a traditional face-to-face exam?
3. List, in your own words, the most important strategies you can use *in* the traditional or online invigilated exam.
4. How might plagiarism be a danger in a 'take home' exam, and how can you avoid it?
5. What are the main things you can do, in terms of writing, to ensure your marker focuses on your key ideas?
6. Think about how you currently deal with stressful situations (not just exams). What do you think is the most effective way for you to deal with stress? What other strategies might be helpful (see further resources below)?
7. How can you manage your thinking to see exams as a positive experience?

Helpful resources

Dealing with stress

This website is designed for school students, but it contains really useful ideas and links. 6 tips to beat final exam stress: http://www.collegefashion.net/college-life/6-tips-to-beat-final-exam-stress

Exam stress: https://www.qld.gov.au/youth/health-looking-after-yourself/mental-health-support-counselling/managing-your-thoughts/exam-stress

Exam preparation

Cengage has a great resource on online exams: https://blog.cengage.com/tips-taking-online-exams

Studying solo: how to prepare for online exams at home: https://www.theguardian.com/education/2020/dec/02/studying-solo-how-to-prepare-for-online-exams-at-home

This resource has links to a specific university strategy, but you will find it is full of excellent advice – read it through to the end. Planning, revision and preparation for online exams: https://www.kent.ac.uk/guides/planning-revision-and-preparation-for-online-exams

Index